W9-ACP-962

The Student Evaluation Standards

THE STUDENT EVALUATION STANDARDS

How to Improve Evaluations of Students

THE JOINT COMMITTEE ON STANDARDS
FOR EDUCATIONAL EVALUATION

Arlen R. Gullickson, Chair

Sponsored by

American Association of School Administrators
American Counseling Association
American Educational Research Association
American Evaluation Association
American Psychological Association
Association for Supervision and Curriculum Development
Canadian Evaluation Society
Canadian Society for the Study of Education
Consortium for Research on Educational Accountability and Teacher Evaluation
Council of Chief State School Officers
National Association of Elementary School Principals
National Association of Secondary School Principals
National Council on Measurement in Education
National Education Association
National Legislative Program Evaluation Society
National School Boards Association

http://jc.wmich.edu/

The Student Evaluation Standards

How to Improve Evaluations of Students

The Joint Committee on Standards
for Educational Evaluation
Arlen R. Gullickson, Chair

A Joint Publication of

For information:

Corwin Press, Inc.
A Sage Publications Company
2455 Teller Road
Thousand Oaks, California 91320
www.corwinpress.com

Sage Publications Ltd.
6 Bonhill Street
London EC2A 4PU
United Kingdom

Sage Publications India Pvt. Ltd.
M-32 Market
Greater Kailash I
New Delhi 110 048 India

JCSEE PR-2003
Approved by the American National Standards Institute as an American National Standard.
Approval date: 6/26/02

Printed in the United States of America

Library of Congress Cataloging-in-Publication Data

Joint Committee on Standards for Educational Evaluation
The student evaluation standards: How to improve evaluations of students / the Joint Committee on Standards for Educational Evaluation; Arlen R. Gullickson, chair; sponsored by American Association of School Administrators . . . [et al.]
p. cm.
Includes bibliographical references and index.
ISBN 0-7619-4662-4 (cloth)
ISBN 0-7619-4663-2 (pbk.)
1. Educational tests and measurements—Standards—United States. 2. American Association of School Administrators. III. Title.
LB3051 .J575 2003
371.26′4—dc21

2002014621

This book is printed on acid-free paper.

02 03 04 05 10 9 8 7 6 5 4 3 2 1

Acquisitions Editor: Faye Zucker
Editorial Assistant: Julia Parnell
Developmental Editor: Tish Davidson
Copy Editor: Liann Lech
Production Editor: Denise Santoyo
Typesetter: C&M Digitals (P) Ltd
Indexer: Kathy Paparchontis
Cover Designer: Michael Dubowe

Table of Contents

Functional Table of Contents

To facilitate study of individual topics, this table lists common evaluation tasks and issues, as well as standards that relate most closely to them.

Planning Evaluations

Communicating and Reporting

Grading

Determining Professional Competence

Developing Policy

Making Evaluative Decisions

Evaluating Technical Issues and Methodology

Ensuring Fairness

Evaluating Students From Diverse Backgrounds

Conducting and Managing Evaluations

Preparing and Developing Professionals

The Joint Committee

Chair

Arlen Gullickson (1998 – present)

James R. Sanders (1988 – 1998)

Vice Chair

Jerry Horn (1998 – 2002)

Arlen Gullickson (1995 – 1998)

Committee Members

Edith Beatty, representing the Association for Supervision and Curriculum Development (ASCD)

Rolf Blank, representing the Council of Chief State School Officers (CCSSO)

Fred Brown and Wayne Rietberg, representing the National Association of Elementary School Principals (NAESP)

Flora Caruthers and David Summers, representing the National Legislative Program Evaluation Society (NLPES)

Timothy Crawford, Glen Cutlip, and Segun Eubanks, representing the National Education Association (NEA)

Jim Cullen, Gwen Keith, and Joan Kruger, representing the Canadian Evaluation Society (CES)

Mark Davison, Ruth Ekstrom, and Jack Naglieri, representing the American Psychological Association (APA)

Darrell Drury and Kevin Hollenbeck, representing the National School Boards Association (NSBA)

Paula Egelson and Todd Rogers, representing the Consortium for Research on Educational Accountability and Teacher Evaluation (CREATE)

Patty McDivitt, representing the American Counseling Association (ACA)

Charles Moore and Jerry Valentine, representing the National Association of Secondary School Principals (NASSP)

Dianna Newman and Wendy Tackett, representing the American Evaluation Association (AEA)

Gary Wegenke, representing the American Association of School Administrators (AASA)

Mark Wilson, representing the American Educational Research Association (AERA)

Robert Wilson, representing the Canadian Society for the Study of Education (CSSE)

Donald Yarbrough, representing the National Council on Measurement in Education (NCME)

Acknowledgments

The contributions of many people and organizations made publication of *The Student Evaluation Standards* possible. The 16 sponsoring organizations for the Joint Committee, the W. K. Kellogg Foundation, and the Western Michigan University Evaluation Center provided financial and in-kind support for this volume. Individuals who contributed to the development of these standards are identified in the lists of support groups in the appendix. The Joint Committee expresses its gratitude to everyone who supported this effort and to all who use the *Standards* to improve evaluations of students and, consequently, student learning and skill.

The Joint Committee takes sole responsibility for any limitations and deficiencies in the *Standards*. Royalties from the sales of this book will be used to promote effective use of the *Standards* and to support Joint Committee development, review, revision, and dissemination activities.

Invitation to Users

The Student Evaluation Standards is the product of a collaborative effort to provide classroom teachers, others who evaluate students, and users of student evaluation information and results with principles and guidelines for assessing and improving student evaluations. The goal was to develop standards to help ensure ethical, useful, feasible, and accurate evaluations of students. These standards must be used, reviewed, and improved as part of the ongoing process to improve and advance the practice of student evaluation.

To promote dissemination and use of these standards, copyright permission is provided to list the summary of the 28 standards as presented in the tear-out card at the back of this book. For example, include it in school policy manuals and course syllabi, and post it on classroom walls. Please cite this book whenever presenting the list.

Joint Committee on Standards for Educational Evaluation. (2003). *The Student Evaluation Standards*. Arlen Gullickson, Chair. Thousand Oaks, CA: Corwin.

If the list is placed on a Web site, we encourage including the Corwin Press Web site (www.corwinpress.com) with the citation.

We invite you to share your experience in using the *Standards* with the Joint Committee. To help with this process, the Committee has prepared a package containing a letter of acknowledgment, information about the review and revision process, and a supply of feedback forms together with directions for their use. The feedback forms request two types of feedback.

The information contained in this Invitation to Users is not part of this American National Standard (ANS) and has not been processed in accordance with ANSI's requirements for an ANS. As such, this Invitation to Users may contain material that has not been subjected to public review or a consensus process. In addition, it does not contain requirements necessary for conformance to the standard.

First, to help us understand the context in which the evaluations were conducted, we would like you to

a. Describe the roles and responsibilities of the people—classroom teacher, students, parents—involved in the evaluation or evaluation system being examined
b. Provide a summary of the evaluation or evaluation system, including how you applied the standards
c. Describe the assessment methods and, if possible, provide copies of the instruments that were used

Given the context, we would like you to

a. Describe any problems you had in applying individual standards
b. Describe any conflicts you found among the standards and how you resolved them
c. Identify terms or terminology that were not clear to you
d. Identify important topics or areas that you feel should be, but are not, covered by the *Standards*

You can obtain a copy of the package by contacting the Joint Committee at

The Joint Committee on Standards for Educational Evaluation
The Evaluation Center
Western Michigan University
Kalamazoo, MI 49008–5237

or from the Internet at

http://jc.wmich.edu/

The Joint Committee also developed a Checklist for Applying the Standards that you may attach to evaluation plans, reports, or other student evaluation materials that you reviewed with *The Student Evaluation Standards*. A copy of this form is provided in Resource B; you may make as many copies of this form as you need.

Preface

This book presents the first unified, national discussion of how to plan, conduct, use, and judge classroom-based student evaluations. It provides the foundation for more ethical, useful, feasible, and sound evaluation principles, policies, and practices. Publication of *The Student Evaluation Standards* makes several important goals easier. For example,

1. Staff of preservice and in-service programs to teach the best evaluation practices can take advantage of this book and other Joint Committee materials.
2. Teachers and administrators can read this book to develop, strengthen, and reflect on their own expertise.
3. School leaders can use this book as a foundation upon which to develop written policies and guidelines.
4. Students can gain an understanding of their important roles in evaluations and learn how to use evaluations more effectively.
5. Parents can learn how to effectively engage in the evaluation process to assist their children in learning.

The Student Evaluation Standards focuses primarily on student evaluations in classrooms. Some may ask why these standards do not speak directly and extensively to large-scale, high-stakes testing. The Joint Committee chose to direct its efforts to the improvement of the evaluation practices used to guide the learning and progress of students. We believe that improving

---

The information contained in this Preface is not part of this American National Standard (ANS) and has not been processed in accordance with ANSI's requirements for an ANS. As such, this Preface may contain material that has not been subjected to public review or a consensus process. In addition, it does not contain requirements necessary for conformance to the standard.

student evaluation practices will substantially serve the goals and objectives that high-stakes tests attempt to measure. Readers interested in standards addressing large-scale, high-stakes testing should consult the *Standards for Educational and Psychological Testing* (American Educational Research Association, American Psychological Association, & National Council on Measurement in Education [AERA, APA, NCME], 1999).

Many reviewers and field-trial participants have heralded *The Student Evaluation Standards* as a comprehensive and important guide for teachers, administrators, parents, and students. Some reviewers have suggested that we consider shortening the book. They argued that teachers do not have the time for more than a few standards accompanied by brief explanations that are presented on a few pages. The Joint Committee believes that the issues addressed in student evaluations are complex, and that it is not appropriate to make the *Standards* inaccurately simplistic. We have tried to ensure readability for both teachers and lay audiences. Sections such as the Functional Table of Contents are intended to enhance access to the *Standards*, and it is the intention of the Committee to encourage development of further support materials. We trust that those who use this book will find the material to be useful and worthwhile.

Member volunteers from the Joint Committee's 16 sponsoring organizations and more than 100 other individuals contributed thousands of hours to produce and test *The Student Evaluation Standards*. Their unselfish contributions attest to the importance we all attach to the central role that sound evaluation plays in student learning.

Taken together, the 28 standards provide a working philosophy for student evaluations. They define the Joint Committee's conception of the principles that should guide and govern student evaluations, and they offer practical suggestions for observing these principles.

Created in 1975, the Joint Committee on Standards for Educational Evaluation is a nonprofit organization incorporated exclusively for developing evaluation standards and promoting their use. Since 1989, the Joint Committee has been a member organization of the American National Standards Institute and follows ANSI procedures in developing, revising, and approving standards. It is the only educational organization developing ANSI-approved evaluation standards. The Committee performs its work on behalf of its constituents, namely, the people and groups involved in conducting educational evaluations and using the results of educational evaluations. *The Student Evaluation Standards* is the third set of standards developed by the Joint Committee. The previous two sets are *The Personnel Evaluation Standards*, published in 1988, and *The Program Evaluation Standards*, published in 1994. The rich history of the Joint Committee is recounted briefly in the Preface to *The Program Evaluation Standards*.

Perhaps the feature that most distinguishes this set of standards from the Joint Committee's standards for program and personnel evaluations is that these standards are meant to serve persons who do not have substantial training in evaluation. In spite of differences in the audiences for the three books, the ties among them are many and strong. Indeed, all three books of standards have the improvement of education as their goal. Their commonality is evident in the following paragraph, which was adapted from *The Program Evaluation Standards* (1994):

> The *Standards* is an effort to provide guidance to effective evaluation. The *Standards* alone cannot guarantee or ensure the quality of any evaluation. Sound evaluation will require the exercise of professional judgment in order to adequately apply the *Standards* to a particular setting. The *Standards* is intended to reflect best practice at the time it was written. The Joint Committee recognizes that, as professional practice changes and the professional knowledge base concerning evaluation develops over time, the *Standards* itself will need to be revised to address those new developments. However, the Joint Committee is confident that the *Standards* will continue to lead to useful, feasible, ethical, and sound student evaluations, and that these evaluations will, in turn, contribute significantly to the betterment of education in diverse classroom settings.

Reference

American Educational Research Association. American Psychological Association, & National Council on Measurement in Education. (1999). *Standards for educational and psychological testing.* Washington, DC: American Educational Research Association.

About the Author

Arlen R. Gullickson, Ph.D., is Director of The Evaluation Center and Professor of Education at Western Michigan University, Kalamazoo, Michigan. Since 1998 he has served as chair of The Joint Committee on Standards for Educational Evaluation. His and the Center's work focuses on improving the theory and practice of evaluation. His writing includes books, chapters, and articles on evaluation. Much of his writing has focused on teacher preparation and practices for evaluation of students and on improving teachers' assessment practices. He directs an annual national institute on evaluation and provides extensive support information for evaluation through the Center's Web site at http://evaluation.mich.edu.

The Corwin Press logo—a raven striding across an open book—represents the happy union of courage and learning. We are a professional-level publisher of books and journals for K-12 educators, and we are committed to creating and providing resources that embody these qualities. Corwin's motto is "Success for All Learners."

Introduction

Evaluation of students is central to student learning in every school and classroom. Without evaluation, we do not know if learning has taken place, nor can we plan for future learning opportunities. Several questions naturally arise from this need for evaluative information. Where in the instructional processes should assessments occur? How frequently should they occur? What questions should be asked and answered? How is information used individually and collectively to make decisions that direct student learning and behavior? Who has the right to access and use this information? These questions address only a few of the evaluative elements of strong learning programs.

We know that for learning to be most effective, students must actively participate in the assessment process and effectively apply the resulting information in making their decisions. We expect teachers working with students in the lower grades of elementary school to conduct the evaluations and lead all aspects of the evaluation process. However, as students grow older, we expect them to play a larger role in their evaluations. In order to assume this role, students must understand the assessment process. Their understanding is highly dependent upon the evaluation knowledge and skills of their teachers.

To effectively serve student learning requires that all involved parties understand and apply sound student evaluation principles. The standards in this book provide a guide for those who seek to learn more about student

---

The information contained in this Introduction is not part of this American National Standard (ANS) and has not been processed in accordance with ANSI's requirements for an ANS. As such, this Introduction may contain material that has not been subjected to public review or a consensus process. In addition, it does not contain requirements necessary for conformance to the standard.

evaluations, those planning evaluations, and those who wish to judge the quality of student evaluations currently occurring in the classroom.

Because student evaluation is a large and complex endeavor, no single book can offer all the information that can and should be learned on the topic. For example, the *Standards for Educational and Psychological Testing* (AERA, APA, NCME, 1999) provides research-based, practical guidelines addressing all aspects of standardized testing. *The Student Evaluation Standards* provides a springboard for learning about student evaluation. It identifies key ideas and topics and sets forth expected practices for the conduct of student evaluations. It also provides methods or guidelines for teachers, students, parents/guardians, administrators, and other interested people to judge the quality of student evaluations.

The focus of this book at the classroom level stems from the belief that strong student learning requires consistent, persistent—indeed, daily—attention to effectively gathering, analyzing, and using evaluation information to guide student learning. Sound student evaluations presume the need for substantial assessment skills on the part of the evaluator to deal effectively with a wide range of issues that arise when conducting a student evaluation. Examples of these issues are listed below:

- Defining and explaining the role of evaluation
- Determining the roles of the student, parents/guardians, and the teacher in an evaluation
- Selecting or identifying the methods to be used to collect evaluation information
- Determining how to combine the results and findings from the various assessments used
- Determining the reporting process
- Implementing follow-up of evaluation findings

This book sets forth principles that represent a national and international consensus of what is most important to sound student evaluations. These principles have been developed, reviewed, and agreed upon by the members of the Joint Committee on Standards for Educational Evaluation. Committee members represent 16 major education organizations and, therefore, embody virtually all the varied areas and levels of education. Members of these organizations and nonaffiliated individuals have read, reviewed, and tested these standards. Hundreds of people have directly influenced the written statements provided here. *These standards are certified as American National Standards for the evaluation of students.*

The Student Evaluation Standards presents and elaborates 28 standards for use in classrooms in elementary and secondary schools and tertiary institutions that identify and promote sound student evaluation practices. The standards are intended to facilitate thoughtful dialogue about the appropriate practice of student evaluation. They can help users confront the political and practical realities of the evaluation process, raising such questions as who establishes the criteria for judging the student and who mediates when charges of an unfair or unsound student evaluation are made. They address difficult issues such as educator biases, conflicts of interest, and student cheating. They stimulate thought about such issues as how often and for what purposes students should be evaluated, the qualifications required to evaluate students, access to evaluation information, and a student's right to privacy of evaluation findings. Most importantly, these standards help educators and other stakeholders to know when their student evaluation practices are on track, properly serving student learning, and when they need to be revised.

The standards require that student evaluations be ethical, fair, useful, feasible, and accurate. The Joint Committee recommends that teachers at all levels and others who evaluate students adopt this book as their primary reference for developing, assessing, improving, and implementing institutional policies and teacher practices for evaluating students. The Joint Committee also recommends that these standards be used in conjunction with *The Program Evaluation Standards* (Joint Committee on Standards for Educational Evaluation, 1994) and *The Personnel Evaluation Standards* (Joint Committee on Standards for Educational Evaluation, 1988), which focus on educational programs and personnel, the other two key ingredients in strong student learning.

Intended Audiences

The Student Evaluation Standards is for people who conduct or use student evaluations. These standards are intended especially for use at the classroom level. They have been written to help teachers and others who evaluate students plan and conduct sound, trustworthy evaluations and report the results of these evaluations in an appropriate, accurate, and credible manner. For many teachers, this book will provide their first opportunity to effectively evaluate their own student evaluation practices and will serve as a link to resources that can better prepare them to properly conduct their evaluations.

The standards also are intended to help students, parents/guardians (and others with a legitimate right to know) judge and comment on plans for evaluations. The standards will help them understand the assessment and evaluation processes and decide whether to accept or reject evaluation results, findings, and recommendations for follow-up actions. In this way, those affected by the evaluation can play constructive support roles in the evaluation process. The standards will assist school administrators and school board members in identifying strengths and weaknesses in their evaluation practices, so that evaluations can be improved. These standards can also help university professors improve their evaluations of their own students. For professors teaching students who will become teachers, use of the standards to improve student evaluations in their own classrooms provides valuable demonstrations and mentoring. These standards are also intended to help those who provide continuing education and in-service workshops for practicing teachers. Although not exhaustive, these examples suggest the range of individuals who will find these standards useful.

Need for Student Evaluation Standards

To educate students effectively, educators must use the findings from student evaluations to determine what each student knows and can do competently and what must be done to further develop and encourage the student's educational development. Appropriate student evaluations help all who are engaged in the educational process make better decisions. These evaluation standards provide sound bases for helping teachers think about and construct evaluations to serve instruction and help students meet the content standards.

Sound evaluations help students know what content and skills they have mastered and where they have deficiencies. Students and their parents/guardians need evaluative information to help them set goals and expectations, make decisions about what to study, and formulate plans for the future. They also will use evaluative findings to identify topics in need of remedial follow-up work.

Teachers need evaluation results to assist them in revising and improving classroom instruction and to identify students who need extra help and supplemental resources. Teachers use evaluation results to plan future instruction and advise students on what courses to take and on career planning.

School counselors use evaluation results to help identify at-risk students and assist all students with career planning. School psychologists evaluate students to determine their need for access to special programs. Admission officers at tertiary institutions (universities, colleges, community colleges, and institutes of technology) use grades and grade point averages to admit students, identify scholarship winners, and advise students on what program to pursue and what courses to take.

The range of uses outlined above indicates that the need for feasible, practical student evaluations that are fair, ethical, useful, and accurate is pervasive, important, and multifaceted. Evaluation results and findings that are incorrect or unsound, or evaluation conclusions that are meaningless or unjustified, are likely to be detrimental to a student's progress and future development. Adherence to the standards helps minimize the chance of an evaluation negatively influencing a student's progress and educational development.

Definitions

To guide the development of the standards, the Joint Committee has defined certain key concepts. Because of their importance, these definitions are highlighted in the following box. Other terms used in the standards are defined in the Glossary provided at the back of this book.

Assessment: The process of collecting information about a student to aid in decision making about the student's progress and development.

Assessment method: A strategy or technique teachers and others who evaluate students may use to acquire evaluation information.

Evaluation: The systematic investigation and determination of the worth or merit of an object. In this book, the term *student* will be used generically to refer to the object of the evaluation.

Evaluator: Used in this book to refer to teachers, guidance counselors, school psychologists, and others who evaluate students.

Measurement: The process of assigning numbers or categories to performance according to specified rules.

Metaevaluation: An evaluation of an evaluation.

Stakeholder: Any person legitimately involved in or affected by the evaluation, for example, students, their parents/guardians, teachers, guidance counselors, school psychologists, and others who make decisions that affect the student's education.

Standard: A principle mutually agreed to by people engaged in the professional practice of evaluation that, if met, will enhance the quality and fairness of an evaluation.

Student: Any person who is engaged in formal study, especially in classroom settings, and under the direction of a teacher or other supervisor.

Teacher: A person responsible for instruction and evaluation of students at a preschool, elementary school, secondary school, or tertiary institution.

Nature of the Standards

This book contains a set of standards that speaks to the responsible conduct and use of student evaluations in the classroom. These standards do not specify procedures to be used in student evaluation, for example, specific assessment methods, data processing, or data analysis. Rather, *The Student Evaluation Standards* provides a framework for designing, conducting, and judging student evaluations. As such, the *Standards* is not intended to replace textbooks, manuals, and handbooks concerned with student evaluation. Instead, it should be used in tandem with such materials, helping, for example, to identify what evaluation techniques and skills should be learned and employed.

The Joint Committee cautions that the individual standards are not equally applicable in all evaluations. Professional judgment must be used to identify which standards are most appropriate in each situation. Users of the *Standards* should weigh the relevance of each standard in context and then decide which standards should be accorded the most importance. These decisions should be documented for later reference. To assist in identifying the most important standards for a given situation, a Functional Table of Contents is provided at the beginning of this book. This table helps evaluators gain a comprehensive understanding of the many evaluation facets embedded in central evaluation questions and concerns.

The Functional Table of Contents is organized into 11 sections that correspond to major components of evaluations (e.g., planning evaluations, grading, communicating, and reporting) and issues in student evaluations (e.g., developing policy, ensuring fairness, evaluating students from diverse backgrounds, preparing and developing professionals).

The Joint Committee recognizes that there is overlap among the different standards. This is a result of the complex evaluation processes involved and the strong relationships among the various evaluation issues addressed. These overlaps are intended to help readers see the many and varied relationships and nuances important to understanding and resolving student evaluation problems.

The Student Evaluation Standards was developed for use in the United States. It may or may not be appropriate for use in other countries. The Joint Committee has based its work on American ideals, laws, and education systems and has used examples that are familiar in the United States. We appreciate the useful reviews and suggestions from colleagues in other countries, and two of our members are from Canada. We intend to contribute to continued international exchange in student evaluation; however, we have not tried to develop standards that fit the laws, systems, and circumstances of other countries.

No attempt was made to directly address the substantial and important area of standardized testing as it pertains to matters such as school reform and statewide accountability. The standards do address standardized tests as they relate to decisions for guiding student instruction in day-to-day learning and development. Those with an interest in the larger issues raised by standardized testing are directed to other reference sources such as the *Standards for Educational and Psychological Testing* (AERA, APA, NCME, 1999), *The Program Evaluation Standards* (Joint Committee on Standards for Educational Evaluation, 1994), and *The Personnel Evaluation Standards* (Joint Committee on Standards for Educational Evaluation, 1988).

Organizational Content of the Standards

The 28 standards contained in *The Student Evaluation Standards* are organized around four important attributes of sound evaluation practice: *propriety, utility, feasibility,* and *accuracy*. The Joint Committee believes that these four attributes are necessary and sufficient for sound and fair evaluations of students. Although standards may strengthen more than one attribute, each has been placed in the group that reflects its principal emphasis in promoting sound evaluations.

PROPRIETY STANDARDS

The propriety standards are intended to facilitate protection of the rights of individuals affected by an evaluation. Student evaluations affect people in many ways. Students are most directly affected, but secondary effects can be seen on parents/guardians, teachers, and other stakeholders. These standards promote sensitivity to and warn against unlawful, unscrupulous, unethical, and inept actions by those who conduct evaluations.

Propriety standards require that evaluators understand and obey laws concerning matters such as student-parent rights, privacy, access to information, and the protection of human subjects. They charge those who conduct evaluations to respect these rights and to act in the best interests of students.

The seven standards in this category are Service to Students, Appropriate Policies and Procedures, Access to Evaluation Information, Treatment of Students, Rights of Students, Balanced Evaluation, and Conflict of Interest.

UTILITY STANDARDS

The utility standards guide student evaluations so that they will be informative, timely, and influential. They require evaluators to be clear about the purposes of the evaluation and to be forthright about how and by whom the results will be used. Findings should be available to appropriate audiences in a clear and timely fashion. In addition, the evaluator is responsible for helping those who use student evaluation results to make the best possible use of this information to benefit students.

The seven standards included in this category are Constructive Orientation, Defined Users and Uses, Information Scope, Evaluator Qualifications, Explicit Values, Effective Reporting, and Follow-Up.

FEASIBILITY STANDARDS

The feasibility standards recognize that student evaluations are conducted in a dynamic, real-world setting and can be affected by many environmental factors. For example, the choice of assessment method or procedures, political factors, and resource constraints all can affect the quality of evaluations. Student evaluations should be conducted in practical ways, fit within the constraints of a particular setting, and use no more resources than necessary to produce the needed results.

The three standards included in this category are Practical Orientation, Political Viability, and Evaluation Support.

ACCURACY STANDARDS

The accuracy standards determine whether an evaluation has produced sound information. Student evaluations must be technically adequate and as complete as possible to allow sound judgments to be made. The evaluation methodology should be appropriate to the purpose of the evaluation and the students being evaluated.

The 11 standards included in this category are Validity Orientation, Defined Expectations for Students, Context Analysis, Documented Procedures, Defensible Information, Reliable Information, Bias Identification and Management, Handling Information and Quality Control, Analysis of Information, Justified Conclusions, and Metaevaluation.

FORMAT

The Standards follows a format intended to elaborate on the standard and to facilitate understanding of the principle. The following content describes and elaborates each standard:

Descriptor: A descriptive title for each standard; for example, Constructive Orientation.

Standard: A definition expressed in a sentence with two parts. The first part identifies the standard in the form of a "should" statement. The second part justifies the standard and is introduced by the expression "so that." For example, the Constructive Orientation standard (**P1**) is stated as follows:

> Evaluations of students should promote sound educational principles, fulfillment of instructional missions, and effective student work, so that the educational needs of students are served.

Overview: A conceptual introduction that provides a general understanding of the standard. The Overview is presented in three parts: Explanation, Rationale, and Caveats.

The explanation defines key terms in the standard statement, shows their logical relationship, and makes the standard statement clear and understandable. The rationale provides a justification for the importance of the standard and for its inclusion. The caveats identify special conditions or warnings pertinent to the standard.

Guidelines: A list of procedural suggestions intended to help evaluators and other stakeholders meet the requirements of the standard. The guidelines are strategies for avoiding mistakes in applying the standard. They should not be considered exhaustive or mandatory, but rather as procedures to be followed when they are judged potentially helpful and feasible.

Common Errors: A list of errors associated with the standard. Common errors may be associated with many circumstances and, if not addressed, may compromise the evaluation.

Illustrative Case: One or more illustrations, based on actual student evaluations, of how the standard might be applied. Each case includes a description of a setting; a situation where the standard is or is not met; and a discussion, where needed, of corrective actions that should lead to compliance with the standard. The corrective actions discussed are only illustrative and are not intended to encompass all possible corrective actions.

Supporting Documentation: Selected references provided to assist the reader in further study of the principle stated in the standard.

Organization of the Book

A discussion of how to apply the standards to real-life situations follows this introduction. The main part of the book consists of the full explication of the 28 standards, grouped according to emphasis on propriety, utility, feasibility, and accuracy. The book ends with a glossary, a list of individuals who participated in the development of *The Student Evaluation Standards*, a checklist form to use when applying the standards, and a summary list of the 28 standards.

References

American Educational Research Association, American Psychological Association, & National Council on Measurement in Education. (1999). *Standards for educational and psychological testing.* Washington, DC: American Educational Research Association.

Joint Committee on Standards for Educational Evaluation. (1988). *The personnel evaluation standards.* Thousand Oaks, CA: Corwin.

Joint Committee on Standards for Educational Evaluation. (1994). *The program evaluation standards* (2nd Ed.). Thousand Oaks, CA: Corwin.

Applying the Standards

Regardless of whether you are a teacher, professor, student, parent, administrator, school board member, legislator, or otherwise interested in student evaluations, the Joint Committee suggests five steps in applying the standards:

1. Become very familiar with the standards.
2. Clarify your purpose(s) for applying the standards.
3. Review and select one or more appropriate standards.
4. Apply the standards that you have selected.
5. Based on your application of the standards, decide on and implement a course of action.

As part of the development of *The Student Evaluation Standards*, more than 60 field testers followed the above five steps and applied the standards to a student evaluation situation with which they were familiar. The majority of field testers were actual classroom teachers who applied the standards to improve their own student evaluation practices. Other field testers were administrators interested in designing or improving district policy, college students reviewing how they were evaluated, and professors teaching preservice education courses who reviewed student learning about classroom assessment as well as their own student evaluation practices.

The following sections present each of these five steps in greater detail, illustrated by an extended case example modified from the field trial reports.

The information contained in this section, Applying the Standards, is not part of this American National Standard (ANS) and has not been processed in accordance with ANSI's requirements for an ANS. As such, this section may contain material that has not been subjected to public review or a consensus process. In addition, it does not contain requirements necessary for conformance to the standard.

In this extended case example, an elementary school teacher metaevaluates her own student evaluation practices in the context of a districtwide, second-grade science assessment. (Metaevaluation is the evaluation of a student evaluation or some aspect of the student evaluation.) Each section provides more detail about the specific step and uses this one case to illustrate the teacher's experience in applying the standards.

Step 1: Becoming Familiar With the Standards

The first requirement for applying the standards is to become very familiar with them. One way to become familiar with the standards is simply to read the book. However, there are as many ways to read and use *The Student Evaluation Standards* as there are individual readers. For example, you may want to begin with the case illustrations accompanying each standard. These show how knowledge of the standards can change the way educators and others think about and practice student evaluation. They present realistic challenges that teachers and others face when they set about implementing student evaluation policies and procedures. Or you may want to read all the standard statements first and think about their applicability to your own interests and purposes.

As you become more familiar with the standards, it is important to begin applying them to your thinking about student evaluations. Depending on your specific student evaluation situations, you may find some standards more useful initially. As you apply and reflect on the standards, your expertise in using them will grow and you will begin to understand how they are interconnected and complement each other.

A final suggestion about how to become more familiar with the standards is to attend classes or workshops on how to use them. You can contact the Joint Committee at its Web site to get more information about qualified workshops and workshop leaders. You can also form users groups in your school or community and share your efforts to apply the standards to common situations.

Step 1: Specific Case Application
In the case example selected from the field trials, Ms. C, an elementary school teacher, became familiar with *The Student Evaluation Standards* through in-service professional development. She and the other teachers in her group had access to a prepublication draft of *The Student Evaluation Standards.* They read and

discussed the standards with their group leader and applied selected standards to an instructional activity of their choosing. As Ms. C worked on applying the standards, she became more familiar with them and discovered more ways that application of the standards could be helpful.

Step 2: Clarifying the Purpose(s) for Applying the Standards

The second step in applying the standards, after you have become familiar with them, is to decide what you want to achieve by applying them in your situation. For example, educators can use *The Student Evaluation Standards* for many specific purposes falling under the general goal of improving student evaluation practices, procedures, and policies. Teachers often want to improve the usefulness or the fairness of specific classroom assessments. Similarly, administrators may be interested in improving the general utility of their district procedures as well as specific classroom assessments, grading, and reporting. Students and their parents may be interested in how fair and accurate their own evaluations are. Lead teachers and other teacher educators may be interested in using the standards to enhance beginning teachers' ability to design and implement the most useful, proper, feasible, and accurate classroom evaluation practices. There are many specific purposes the standards can serve, but in general, they are designed to help improve the value of student evaluations to the students themselves and other members of the educational community.

How do teachers and others go about clarifying their purpose(s) in applying the standards? In the example that follows, Ms. C began with a detailed description of the educational setting and the assessment situation that she wanted to improve. As often happens, she began with a general purpose, which changed and became more detailed as she progressed with the application.

Step 2: Specific Case Application

Ms. C chose to metaevaluate an assessment in the districtwide second-grade science curriculum. In this assessment, students individually designed a graph representing characteristics of an "animal" of their choosing. She described the situation as follows:

(Continues)

(Continued)

> *One of the district goals for the North Central Association process is on graphing data. We want students to be able to make a graph and be able to answer questions concerning it. Thus, many of our districtwide math and science assessments deal with graphing. Students are given this Life Science Assessment piece following the unit completion. I use the assessment to assess the students' understanding of the material studied and their graphing ability.*
>
> *During the summer, our district studies all of the required assessment pieces that were taken. They disaggregate the test data by race, gender, and socioeconomic status in order to set new school improvement goals or improve on ones already set.*

The student-developed graphs served as a focal point for generating classroom questions about animals with similar characteristics. Ms. C noted that the Life Science Assessment addressed the students' understanding of mammals, birds, fish, amphibians, and reptiles. Second graders were required to have a good understanding of these animal groups and to be able to identify animals from each category.

The students appeared to enjoy the mechanics (drawing, coloring, etc.) associated with preparing their animals and graphs. However, they often appeared frustrated as they aligned details in a two-dimensional diagram and attempted to form questions. The students' frustrations served as a catalyst (or need) for Ms. C to want to apply *The Student Evaluation Standards.*

Ms. C began to reflect on the specific purposes with which she wanted the standards to help her. Perhaps they could help her clarify if there were any problems that might create frustration in her students. She decided to use the standards to investigate the quality of the assessment, particularly with regard to problems that might frustrate her students, and to help her improve the assessment in ways that might result in a better experience for the students.

Step 3: Reviewing and Selecting One or More Appropriate Standards

The organization and presentation of the standards are intended to facilitate these steps, especially reviewing and selecting standards for application to specific student evaluation situations. For example, the standards are arranged into four groups according to their focus on propriety, utility, feasibility, and accuracy. Thus, if your purpose in applying the standards has more to do with one of these topics (e.g., focusing on feasibility because of limited resources or time), you may choose to start with standards from just that section. More likely, your purposes will cut across the various focus areas, and you can use the Functional Table of Contents to identify common student evaluation situations and the standards most closely tied to them.

Sometimes, the task of selecting the standard or standards to begin with may seem difficult. As those participating in the field tests noted, there are many standards and so many guidelines. Where does one start, and how should one proceed?

There is no single right way to begin using the standards. Rather, the standards can be used appropriately in many ways. You can begin with the application of one standard and then add others that also seem to address your purpose. If you have considerable time and support and all standards seem pertinent to you, you may try to use all the standards.

Step 3: Specific Case Application

In our case example, Ms. C's situation was fortuitous because of the dedicated time that she had for the application of the standards and the opportunity to discuss her application with others. This professional development situation provided Ms. C with reflective time to choose more than one or two standards to begin with. Ms. C stated the process she followed in selecting standards as follows.

> *I used the* Standards *to help me examine one of our mandated district Life Science Assessments for the second grades. I first looked at the Functional Table of Contents and found the function "Conducting and Managing Evaluations" to use as my guide. Next, I looked at each standard under that function individually. For example, a standard that is listed under "Conducting and Managing Evaluations" is*
>
> **A2. Defined Expectations for Students**
>
> *I turned to that standard in the book and began reading. I first read the Summary of the Standards under*

(Continues)

(Continued)

Accuracy Standards. I found that this particular standard deals with the performance expectations for students and how they should be clearly defined, so that the evaluation results are meaningful. Then I proceeded to read about the standard by looking at the overview, rationale, caveats, guidelines, common errors, and illustrative cases. I continued this process for all of the standards listed under the function "Conducting and Managing Evaluations." There were 19 standards that I looked at closely under this heading. After reading about each standard, I determined if it was relevant or not relevant to my application.

Through that process, Ms. C identified 12 standards that she thought best served this particular teaching/learning context. Then she set about applying them. Selecting the standards she thought would provide the best insights was time-consuming, but it helped her become even more familiar with the standards and resulted in efficient use of her time as she applied them. Later, when she wants to try out more of the standards, she can select and apply them one at a time or in small groups.

Step 4: Using the Selected Standards

How you go about using the standards depends greatly on the purpose(s) that you want the application to serve. For example, if your purpose is primarily to learn about factors that influence the usefulness of student evaluations, you might just read through and reflect on the utility standards. This would be a kind of conceptual use of the standards. However, if your purpose is to improve student evaluation practices in a specific system, you are facing a more demanding, instrumental use of the standards.

The Joint Committee is particularly interested in metaevaluative uses of the standards. Metaevaluation takes place when parents, students, administrators, teachers, or others use the standards to make judgments about the quality of student evaluation practices, policies, or procedures. When educators or other evaluators of students use standards to metaevaluate their own student evaluation practices, policies, or procedures, they are engaged in self-reflective metaevaluation.

Metaevaluation requires accurate investigation and description of all aspects of the student evaluations under review. Before using the standards to metaevaluate a specific student evaluation, you should try to describe the student evaluation by answering the following questions:

- Whose performance is evaluated?
- What knowledge, skills, attitudes, and/or behaviors are evaluated?
- Who will use the findings?
- What decisions will be made or influenced by the evaluation results?
- What types of follow-up actions are students, parents/guardians, and other stakeholders expected to make in response to evaluation results?

If you are engaged in a *formal* metaevaluation or any metaevaluation of an assessment not in your own classroom, you should carefully describe the materials and procedures used. The materials might include copies of the assessment instrument(s) or samples of student work. The procedures might include those related to grading; descriptions of the learning opportunities provided to the students to acquire the expected knowledge, skills, attitudes, and/or behaviors being evaluated; the course syllabus or other descriptions explaining for students the evaluation procedures and how the evaluation fits into the course instruction plan; results and information obtained from each assessment method used to judge the knowledge, skills, attitudes, and/or behaviors acquired by the students; anecdotal records; standardized test results; and a sample report card.

In a formal metaevaluation, you should then use these documents to develop a description of the student evaluation practices. There are numerous questions for you to answer. What information was provided to the students about the evaluation process? How and by whom was the evaluation conducted? What questions were addressed by the evaluation? What data and information were collected? How were the data and information scored, analyzed, interpreted, and reported? How was the evaluation organized, scheduled, managed, and monitored? What follow-up activities occurred?

In a formal metaevaluation, you should examine the description and supporting documents for completeness and sufficient information to apply the standards effectively. For example, certain standards require clear information about the intended uses of the evaluation, the role of the evaluator, the procedures for gathering data, the procedures for checking the reliability and validity of the data, or possible actions to be taken as a result of the evaluation. If the information was simply omitted, you should integrate it into the description. If the information is not available, you should note this and continue with the metaevaluation.

Sometimes, the thoroughness required for formal metaevaluation is too time-consuming for the classroom teacher who needs to improve her own student evaluation practices as quickly and efficiently as possible. Although it is most important to think about and reflect on these questions and considerations in any metaevaluation, it is also important not to spend so much time on initial documentation that no time remains to apply one or more standards.

In our case example, Ms. C is engaged in an informal metaevaluation of her own classroom assessment as a reflective exercise. In the beginning, she reflected on some of the above questions, but did not produce documentation for all of them. As you read and reflect on her case, think about which questions she addresses and why, and whether, in your own situation, you might make different choices about how to begin such an informal, self-reflective metaevaluation.

Step 4: Specific Case Application

In the previous step, Ms. C had identified 12 standards to apply to her specific classroom assessment. In this step, she applied the 12 to yield insights about the student evaluation practices under review. As her responses indicate, the standards served as a "reflection" tool. Sometimes, she judged her evaluation practices to satisfactorily meet the recommendations of specific standards. In other cases, she identified areas needing improvement through applying the standards.

In the following paragraphs, you can read some of her written comments following application of some of the standards. For purposes of this example, we list only 6 of the 12 standards that she applied. To get a better sense of how the various elements of the standards work together, we suggest that you turn to that standard in the book to compare both the description and the guidelines as you read her responses below. You will find that she has directly responded to one or more of the guidelines for each identified standard.

A2. Defined Expectations for Students

Students in my second-grade class have an opportunity to bring prior knowledge and experiences to class. Before we started the unit on Animals, we did a K-W-L. This is a three-step process. Students are asked to identify what they know (K) and what they want to know (W). Following instruction on the topic, they are asked to report what they have learned (L). Students had an opportunity to bring their prior knowledge and talk about it in class. Also, at the opening of the unit, students were told that there would be an assessment given at the end on the material that was presented and discussed in class. A graphing activity is always incorporated into each unit, so children are well aware and actually excited about completing a graph.

When children were given the assessment piece at the end of the unit, we read the directions together. We went through the pieces one at a time and discussed what the expectations were. For this particular test, I broke it up into sections and took three days to complete it.

A week prior to the assessment, students took home a short study guide to look over. Parents should be well aware of the upcoming assessments because they got the study guide and a note in their weekly newsletter. Most parents are very good about looking over the information with their child.

A5. Defensible Information

I used a transparency to show a correct graph for students to use in order to answer the questions. If I had not done this, I would have had to interpret their incorrect answers by looking at how they did their graph. It would have been difficult to score their test. Their answers might have been correct according to their graph, but incorrect according to my grading sheet. The results may not have been consistent with the other second-grade classes in [our school district]. Before I did this, however, I called the other second-grade teachers and told them what I was going to do. They thought it was a good idea and agreed to follow the same procedures. Now our district results should be similar. I graded all of the assessments to make sure that there were consistencies in the scoring. The district has provided a rubric that all second-grade teachers should follow. Their final grade is an average of their graph score and the writing score.

After I read this standard, I realized that I didn't use a variety of assessments that could reach each child's

(Continues)

(Continued)

different learning style. Next year, I plan on giving this assessment but adding another one that might meet other learning styles. I would really like to incorporate some type of writing assessment and a one-on-one assessment piece (orally) next year. This standard really got me thinking quite a bit.

F1. Practical Procedures

I made a list prior to the administration of the assessment. On the first day, the students would need a pencil and some type of coloring devices. On the second day, students needed scissors and glue/paste. On the third day, I would need a transparency and the students would need a pencil. I placed most of these items in a tub with the test, so I was well prepared.

I arranged for my instructional assistant to read the questions to the students on day three. I also arranged for her to sit by one child who has trouble staying on task. I sent home a note with the children to their parents stating how the assessment went and their child's score. I also noted some areas the child had trouble in. I put the actual test in the folder for safekeeping.

We took the test during the mornings on a Tuesday, Wednesday, and Thursday. I wanted to avoid Mondays and Fridays since my children do not do as well. I also did not want to give the test in the afternoon. The students in my class seem to be more focused in the morning hours before lunch. For this test, I even passed out a couple of crackers to students before taking the test to see if that would help. I really didn't see any major difference.

P4. Treatment of Students

I try to always provide an upbeat and exciting learning environment. I never tell the kids that they are taking a "test." I always start by saying that I have a fun activity that they are going to get to show off on. Second graders already start to freeze up if I say the terrible word "test."

When I explained the directions, I tried to be very detailed and descriptive. I stopped often to see if they had any questions or concerns. Throughout the assessment,

I had a couple of children who raised their hands because they did not understand a part. This gave me an opportunity to try to explain it to them a different way. I did have a few children that took a bit longer to finish than the rest of the class. I already had a book on each child's desk, so they started to read when they finished. This was allowed for the other children to take their time and complete the test at their own pace. They did not feel rushed or hurried.

U2. Defined Users and Uses

This assessment helped me in understanding not only how students were classifying animals, but also their ability to construct a graph and interpret it. It helped me to evaluate my teaching methods and improve on certain areas of instruction. A few children did perform poorly on the test. I have had my assistant working with them on certain animal groups and new graphing activities. I will evaluate their progress in the next few days to see if their skills have improved. Without such an assessment, I would not have had such clear evidence of children who were struggling. I do not want to lose any child.

U7. Follow-Up

Students take home notes to their parents that state their scores and areas of difficulty. I also grouped the children who had common difficulties together so they could work with our instructional assistant and concentrate on those specific areas. I will evaluate those students again to see if they have improved. I believe that a couple of them simply needed to work in a small group environment. After I have evaluated those students again, I will send another note or give a phone call to the parents to let them know the progress.

As this example illustrates, Ms. C's informal metaevaluation helped her identify strengths and weaknesses of the districtwide classroom assessment and led her to Step 5, putting together a plan of action.

Step 5: Deciding on and Implementing a Course of Action

The purpose for applying the standards, as stated in Step 2 and as it evolves during the application step, leads naturally to a plan of action. In an informal metaevaluation, like Ms. C's, Step 5 flows naturally from Step 4 and may require little planning or preparation. For example, in applying the standards, Ms. C wanted to modify her routine to be sure that she was prepared on assessment day. She planned to put the necessary items into the tub that she would use to collect the assessment materials. In other situations where specific recommendations are needed, for example, if Ms. C presents to other teachers in the district, a more formal report and plan of action will be needed.

When the purpose for applying the standards is a formal metaevaluation of student evaluation practices, procedures, or policies, Step 5 needs careful attention. During Step 4, you should identify critical issues and develop recommendations for strengthening an evaluation or a series of evaluations, just as Ms. C began to do. Then, in Step 5, you can synthesize the information, formulate overarching conclusions, and create a formal plan to improve the student evaluation.

If you have a written description of the student evaluation that addresses the issues outlined above, you can identify specific aspects of the evaluation to examine for strengths and weaknesses. It is important in Step 5 to identify not only what needs improvement, but also those aspects that need to be maintained as they are. Sometimes, during change processes to fix weaknesses, areas of strength may be undermined, especially if they have not been identified.

Expect numerous areas that need improvement. Order and prioritize those improvement needs. You may organize needed improvements according to key evaluation processes, such as those listed below:

- Developing and selecting assessment method(s)
- Collecting assessment information
- Scoring and judging student performance
- Summarizing and interpreting results
- Reporting evaluation findings
- Following up to apply evaluation judgments

Once you have a list of prioritized strengths and weaknesses, you can develop a general plan for yourself or others to use in improving the student evaluations. As much as possible, the plan should recommend who should do what, when, how, and with what level of support. You can address feasibility issues and what will be needed to improve the student evaluation. You may recommend changes to written policies at the school or district level or call for in-service programs designed to help others improve their evaluation skills, learn about new evaluation procedures, and learn how the use of evaluation findings could benefit their students.

This step of the metaevaluation process needs to be especially sensitive to resources and practical matters. It does little good to set forward an agenda that overburdens the teachers or depends on nonexistent resources for support.

Your implementation plan should also focus on how the changes you suggest can be monitored and metaevaluated in the future. In other words, you are probably embarking on a cycle of metaevaluation that requires periodic review of changes that are tried out in order to continually maintain and, when necessary, improve the accuracy, utility, feasibility, and propriety of the student evaluations. Taking on this task, one step at a time and slowly over the school years, promises better evaluations that much better serve the students and the entire learning community. In the long run, the promise is more and better student learning in response to improved student evaluation practices, procedures, and policies.

Step 5: Specific Case Application

During the field trial process, Ms. C did not complete a formal plan of action. As you noticed in the Step 4 specific application, she did identify strengths and weaknesses, and she formulated some action steps. However, she went back to her school not yet ready to complete a formal plan. First of all, she needed more time to apply more of the standards to see if there were other compelling strengths and weaknesses. She also wanted to confer with her second-grade colleagues to gather more information about the assessment and all the uses made of it. Finally, she was wondering, because this was a district assessment, whether it might be preferable to get others involved in the metaevaluation before putting together a formal plan of action. She decided to put this on the agenda for the districtwide meeting that was coming up. Ms. C closed her report with the following synthesis comment.

> *I have found that the Life Science Assessment that I have given to my second graders might not be as wonderful as I thought previously. I know that I am not reaching each child's learning style with this particular test. Also, I found*

(Continues)

(Continued)

that this assessment is really concentrating on our NCA [North Central Association] goal of graphing abilities. It is not really testing their knowledge of classifying animals. I plan on taking my concerns to our next grade level meeting in hopes of making some districtwide changes to it.

Improvement in student evaluation practices and procedures can result when teachers apply the standards reflectively to their own practices. For example, by applying specific standards, Ms. C was able to evaluate the graphing assessment and identify needed changes. In addition, the standards helped her illuminate how she treated and reported to her students. They helped her focus on how she took into account her students' backgrounds and how she followed up evaluation results. By using *The Student Evaluation Standards,* she both affirmed some of what she was doing and identified areas needing improvement, not only in her assessments, but also in her instructional practices.

In addition to metaevaluating existing assessment practices, most teachers and administrators can also use the *Standards* to design better practices, procedures, and policies in advance of implementation. The more teachers, administrators, and others apply the standards in this reflective way, the more efficient and effective the application of standards will become. In the long run, these efforts have enormous potential to improve the impact of student evaluation practices on student learning and schooling in general.

To facilitate application of selected standards, the Joint Committee prepared a checklist, available in Resource B and on the Joint Committee Web site listed on the title page.

THE STANDARDS

P PROPRIETY STANDARDS

Summary of the Standards

P Propriety Standards The propriety standards help ensure that student evaluations will be conducted legally, ethically, and with due regard for the well-being of the students being evaluated and other persons affected by the evaluation results. These standards are as follows:

- **P1 Service to Students** Evaluations of students should promote sound education principles, fulfillment of institutional missions, and effective student work, so that educational needs of students are served.
- **P2 Appropriate Policies and Procedures** Written policies and procedures should be developed, implemented, and made available, so that evaluations are consistent, equitable, and fair.
- **P3 Access to Evaluation Information** Access to a student's evaluation information should be provided, but limited to the student and others with established legitimate permission to view the information, so that confidentiality is maintained and privacy protected.
- **P4 Treatment of Students** Students should be treated with respect in all aspects of the evaluation process, so that their

dignity and opportunities for educational development are enhanced.

P5 Rights of Students Evaluations of students should be consistent with applicable laws and basic principles of fairness and human rights, so that students' rights and welfare are protected.

P6 Balanced Evaluation Evaluations of students should provide information that identifies both strengths and weaknesses, so that strengths can be built upon and problem areas addressed.

P7 Conflict of Interest Conflicts of interest should be avoided, but if present should be dealt with openly and honestly, so that they do not compromise evaluation processes and results.

P1 Service to Students

STANDARD Evaluations of students should promote sound education principles, fulfillment of institutional missions, and effective student work, so that educational needs of students are served.

Overview

Explanation. A major purpose of student evaluation is to guide students, their parents/guardians, and educators in the students' acquisition of the knowledge, skills, attitudes, and behaviors that they will need as adults to participate in a democratic society. Student evaluations should help students and other stakeholders understand the goals and objectives of instruction and each student's status and progress in relation to these desired outcomes. In addition, student evaluations should help students, parents/guardians, and teachers plan future instruction and, where needed, appropriate follow-up remedial action (see U7, Follow-Up).

Rationale. If a teacher starts with clear and appropriate expectations, plans and implements effective instruction, evaluates student progress accurately, and keeps students believing that important targets are within reach, the teacher will help motivate students to grow and develop. Students are most motivated to learn when their evaluations are clearly aligned with the goals and objectives of instruction and provide information that can be used to design appropriate follow-up actions.

Caveats. In the daily press for accountability, student evaluations can become simply a basis for justifying grades awarded and other accountability decisions. Teachers must ensure that evaluations primarily serve the instruction and learning needs of students and, where appropriate, the teacher's instructional needs.

GUIDELINES

A. Determine learning needs, then plan and conduct evaluations to serve those needs.
B. Be clear about the purposes and uses of the evaluation (see U2, Defined Users and Uses).
C. Promote student evaluation as an integral part of a regular and continuous process for individual improvement (see U1, Constructive Orientation).
D. Ensure that evaluations are aligned with expected learning outcomes and take into account the instruction provided to students (see A1, Validity Orientation).
E. Show students the relationship between evaluation and student learning. Where possible, directly involve them in the process as student evaluators.
F. Inform parents/guardians of the evaluation process to be followed during a reporting period and/or year to help them see how evaluation serves their child's needs (see U6, Effective Reporting).
G. Ensure that the evaluation system provides for alternate procedures for students with disabilities and students whose proficiency in the language of instruction is inadequate for them to respond in the anticipated manner (see A3, Context Analysis; P5, Rights of Students).
H. Ensure that evaluation results and information are reported to students, parents/guardians, and other legitimate users in a form that is understandable and useful to these audiences (see U6, Effective Reporting).

COMMON ERRORS

A. Failing to provide students with sufficient opportunity to demonstrate their knowledge, skills, attitudes, and behaviors
B. Overusing instructional time for accountability-based student evaluations to the detriment of student learning
C. Failing to provide for follow-up actions where their need is indicated by the results of a student evaluation (see U7, Follow-Up)
D. Putting more emphasis on student evaluations as a mechanism to serve school accountability rather than as a way to serve student learning

Illustrative Case 1—Description

Mr. Gomez is a middle school social studies teacher whose approach to instruction has grown increasingly learner-centered. He now insists that his students take responsibility for their own learning. He uses a variety of assessment methods to evaluate each student. These assessments are closely aligned with what the students are expected to learn. Furthermore, students are expected to comment on and account for the marks and comments they receive each time they are evaluated.

The students also are required to complete an annual assessment mandated by the state and local school district. Mr. Gomez helps his students understand the purposes, uses, and timing of all components in this annual assessment. He shows them how each component is learner-centered. This has resulted in a more positive attitude toward what the students formerly thought of as "those stupid tests."

Illustrative Case 1—Analysis

Mr. Gomez's assessment approach places students at the center of evaluation regardless of the source of the assessment (classroom, district, or state). Assessment and evaluation are presented to the students as a continuous process for individual improvement with many and varied opportunities to demonstrate their knowledge and skills. Mr. Gomez does not abandon that approach with the annual mandated state assessment. He takes the time to explain how this assessment is related to what the students have been doing in class throughout the year.

Illustrative Case 2—Description

The goal of Ms. Margolis, an instructor in a university statistics class, was for her students to understand the appropriate use of statistics. She gave homework assignments designed to foster this objective, a mid-term, and a final examination. She graded these materials, and then reported the results to the students. She returned the homework assignments, but not the mid-term or final exam. She wanted to keep the tests secure, so that they could be used again. While students were told their scores on the exams, they were not allowed to review their work or the evaluative judgments she had made.

Illustrative Case 2—Analysis

Ms. Margolis's actions were detrimental to her students. She provided no opportunity for the students to review their mid-term and final exams, so that they could more fully understand their performance. Students lost an opportunity to learn from the instructor's evaluation, as there was no way they could determine what they did and did not know. Ms. Margolis seemed less concerned about student learning than about reducing her workload by eliminating the need to construct new tests. She could have allowed students to review their work under supervised conditions while still keeping the tests secure for future use.

Supporting Documentation

Airasian, P. W. (1997). *Classroom assessment* (3rd ed.). New York: McGraw-Hill.

Cangelosi, J. S. (2000). *Assessment strategies for monitoring student learning.* New York: Addison Wesley Longman.

Linn, R. L., & Gronlund, N. E. (2000). *Measurement and assessment in teaching* (8th ed.). Upper Saddle River, NJ: Prentice Hall.

Marzano, R. J. (1992). *A different kind of classroom: Teaching with the dimensions of learning.* Alexandria, VA: Association for Supervision and Curriculum Development.

Marzano, R. J., Pickering, D., & McTighe, J. (1993). *Assessing student outcomes.* Alexandria, VA: Association for Supervision and Curriculum Development.

Stiggins, R. J. (1997). *Student-centered classroom assessment.* Upper Saddle River, NJ: Prentice Hall.

Author's Note

The cases illustrating each standard are drawn from the experiences of the many contributors to the standards. As such they are grounded in real classroom situations. However, each illustration has been changed in many ways to better address the particular standard and to disguise the local teaching situation. For example, all teacher names are fictitious and grade levels, content areas, and locations were routinely changed.

P2 Appropriate Policies and Procedures

STANDARD Written policies and procedures should be developed, implemented, and made available, so that evaluations are consistent, equitable, and fair.

Overview

Explanation. Well-developed, publicly available written policies define the purposes and procedures for student evaluations. School policies and guidelines should ensure that student evaluations completed by different teachers in different instructional settings are conducted in a consistent, meaningful, and useful way. Examples of issues that should be addressed in written policies include the following:

- Equity and fairness in matters of race and sex
- Allowable alternatives for students with special needs and/or limited language competence
- Student cheating and plagiarism
- Grading and reporting procedures
- How excused and unexcused absences are treated
- Student grievance and appeal procedures
- Confidentiality of student evaluation information
- Skills and qualifications of evaluators

When adhered to, these policies set boundaries that ensure all students are evaluated in a consistent, equitable, and fair manner. Written procedures or guidelines that specify how stakeholders should proceed should accompany each policy statement to clarify application of the policy.

Rationale. Student evaluations must be carried out consistently, equitably, and fairly. Clearly written purposes, criteria, and procedures outlined in public policy statements and guidelines increase the likelihood that

- Performance expectations for students will be understood
- A uniform standard of judgment will be applied
- Evaluations will be fair
- Evaluation results will be trusted and used

Student evaluations conducted without a written policy and accompanying procedures risk being poorly performed; variable across teachers, courses, and time; susceptible to misuse and abuse, and without opportunity for review or recourse.

Caveats. No matter how clear and defensible policies and procedures are, they will never be free of the need for interpretation. Policies and procedures need to be reviewed and revised periodically as conditions, applications, objectives, and values change.

GUIDELINES

A. Obtain consensus on policies and procedures from teachers, administrators, parents/guardians, and, where appropriate, students.

B. Include evaluation policies in student handbooks sent home to parents/guardians. These policies should explain the following:
   - The evaluation process
   - Expectations for students
   - Rights of students and parents/guardians
   - How disagreements between student and teacher on evaluation matters will be resolved
   - How scores will be aggregated and final grades determined
   - How results of evaluations will be reported to students and other stakeholders
   - How results will be used at the classroom and school level

C. Identify roles and responsibilities for all persons involved in or affected by the evaluation.

D. Ensure that policies and procedures are consistent with applicable laws and with basic principles of fairness and human rights (see P5, Rights of Students).

E. Ensure that policies set at the classroom level align with policies set at the department and school levels.

F. Monitor adherence to written policies and procedures.

G. Establish a process for periodic review and revision of written policies and procedures.

H. Develop clear and effective policies regarding student behavior in evaluation situations, addressing such issues as plagiarism, use of other students' work, sharing of information, and cheating. Establish consequences for unacceptable behavior. Define the teachers' responsibilities and authority, as well as the responsibilities and rights of students and their parents/guardians where appropriate (see A5, Defensible Information).

COMMON ERRORS

A. Writing policies and procedures that are vague, too broad, or confusing
B. Establishing policies after evaluations have been conducted
C. Applying policies retroactively, such as changing the evaluation system in midcourse, without accounting for previous evaluation results and findings
D. Promoting policies without procedures and procedures without policies

Illustrative Case 1—Description

Torrey Pine High School had just embraced site-based management and was still in the process of developing new policies and procedures when school started in early September. The management team, consisting of a representative from each department, completed development of the new schoolwide student evaluation policy and provided it to all departments for implementation by mid-November. However, no operational procedures were developed to implement the policy, nor was the new policy discussed with the full teaching staff.

At the beginning of the school year, Mr. Jones, the science teacher, told his students that he would test them using multiple-choice tests that came with the teacher's edition of the textbook. He told the students that there would be a test at the end of each chapter and that their scores on these chapter tests would determine their semester grades. Mr. Jones thought that because these tests could be objectively scored, the results would be fair and free from bias that might occur in subjective scoring of performance assessments.

Wan Lee, a student in Mr. Jones' class who had excellent laboratory skills, received a D in the first reporting period. His parents complained to the principal that Mr. Jones' assessment system was too narrow and did not meet the new school evaluation policy that indicated a variety of assessments should be used. They thought their son's evaluation should have included an assessment of his laboratory skills.

Following school policy, the principal sent the issue to the school management team for resolution. However, the management team did not know how to proceed with the complaint. They lacked specific procedures to follow when a complaint was filed. Consequently, resolution of the problem, which went in favor of Wan Lee, became confused and at times difficult, with Mr. Jones pitted against the student, his parents, and the management team.

Illustrative Case 1—Analysis

Development of a strong schoolwide policy on student evaluation is commendable. As is often the case, the development of the policy occurred after the start of the school year. In the case of Torrey Pine High School, the policy went into effect midway through the semester.

Two mistakes resulted. First, teachers were not properly informed of the new policy nor asked to ensure compliance with it. Taking this step probably would have caused Mr. Jones to change his evaluation practices and might have averted the parental complaint and subsequent grievance process.

Second, the policy itself was flawed, because it did not provide procedural steps for handling complaints. It also failed to provide procedures for implementing the new policy. For example, delaying implementation of the new evaluation policy until the beginning of the next term would have given teachers adequate time to change their evaluation procedures and inform students of the changes. As implemented, the new policy placed Mr. Jones in an untenable position, because his evaluation procedures failed to adequately meet the new policy. However, the policy was not in effect when he prepared and conducted most of his evaluations. In addition, rather than having the new policy explained in staff discussions, Mr. Jones learned of the new policy from a student complaint when it was too late for him to modify his evaluation procedures.

Illustrative Case 2—Description

Polly has severely limited vision. She is enrolled in Joan Stephenson's class at Monroe Elementary School. With the use of aids, Polly is able to read most print materials, although she takes much longer to do so than most students her age. Ms. Stephenson's evaluation policy states "All students are to be treated equally in assessment situations."

Ms. Stephenson knew that she would need to modify the assessment procedures for Polly. She knew that Polly would need more time than the other students to complete her tests and also might need materials in larger print or to have the test questions read aloud to her. Thus, Polly would not be assessed in the same way as the other students in the class.

Ms. Stephenson discussed her policy and her dilemma with other teachers, the counselor, and the principal. She checked the relevant laws, regulations, and school district policies about students with disabilities and found that her evaluation policy was not in accordance with them. She realized that where her policy said "equally," it should have said "fairly." Therefore, she changed her policy to allow modifications where necessary. She explained the changes to all her students and their parents/guardians, and shared her experience with the principal and teachers in the school. As a result, a schoolwide policy with accompanying procedures was developed for assessing students who could not respond to an assessment method as administered.

Illustrative Case 2—Analysis

Ms. Stephenson recognized the need to alter what she initially believed to be a fair student evaluation policy. Although having Polly complete an assessment in the same time or without enlarged print would be the same as for the other students, it would unfairly disadvantage Polly. She would not be able to show what she knew and could do.

Checking with other teachers, the counselor, and the principal about what they thought should be done and confirming existing regulations about disabled students helped to focus Ms. Stephenson on the difference in meaning between equal and equitable. Changing her policy and procedures and sharing the changes with her students and their parents/guardians were appropriate actions. Likewise, discussing the policy with the other teachers helped them to better understand the need for clearly worded policies and procedures.

Supporting Documentation

American Federation of Teachers, National Council on Measurement in Education, & National Education Association. (1990). *Standards for teacher competence in educational assessment of students*. Washington, DC: National Council on Measurement in Education.

American Educational Research Association, American Psychological Association, & National Council on Measurement in Education. (1999). *Standards for educational and psychological testing*. Washington, DC: American Educational Research Association.

Joint Advisory Committee. (1993). *Principles for fair student assessment practices for education in Canada*. Edmonton, Alberta, Canada: University of Alberta, Centre for Research in Applied Measurement and Evaluation.

Joint Committee on Testing Practices. (1998). *Code of fair testing practices in education.* Washington, DC: American Psychological Association.

Joint Committee on Testing Practices. (1999). *Test takers' rights and responsibilities.* Washington, DC: American Psychological Association.

National Education Association. (1992). *Handbook: Ethical standards for teachers' relations with pupils.* Washington, DC: Author.

Scriven, M. (1991). *Evaluation thesaurus* (4th ed.). Newbury Park, CA: Sage.

U.S. Department of Education, Office for Civil Rights. (2000). *The use of tests as part of high-stakes decision-making for students: A resource guide for educators and policy-makers.* Washington, DC: Author. Retrieved May 17, 2002, from http://www.ed.gov/offices/OCR/testing/.

P3 Access to Evaluation Information

STANDARD Access to a student's evaluation information should be provided, but limited to the student and others with established legitimate permission to view the information, so that confidentiality is maintained and privacy protected.

Overview

Explanation. Access to student evaluation information must be carefully protected. First, the appropriate users of evaluation information should be established (see U2, Defined Users and Uses). Students and, where applicable, their parents/guardians are entitled to reports that present assessment information and evaluation findings in a clearly understandable form, so that they can use this information to address the student's educational development (see P1, Service to Students). Others with a legitimate need for the evaluation information (e.g., school principal, school counselor, school psychologist, or social worker) should be authorized to inspect and use evaluative information in order to assess and make decisions. Such disclosure is essential if student evaluations are to be influential in furthering each student's learning and development.

Second, regardless of the user of the evaluation findings, confidentiality must be maintained and respected. At the classroom level, teachers should ensure that report cards are provided only to the student and the student's parents/guardians. Teachers should not share evaluation information about one student with another student or other parents/guardians.

Release of student evaluation information to serve legitimate needs must be controlled to safeguard the student and others engaged in the educational process. For example, researcher requests to analyze student records and achievement information should be approved only under carefully constrained conditions. These requests must meet school policy guidelines (see P2, Appropriate Policies and Procedures). When full access for research is requested (i.e., including student identification), student and, where applicable, parent/guardian consent must be obtained before access is granted.

Rationale. Stakeholders need to have ready access to student evaluation information to serve student learning and other instructional and developmental needs. At the same time, providing such access may result in harm to the student, damage to student-teacher or other important relationships, and litigation. When the need for access and confidentiality are at odds, the safety and respect of the student should be the overriding concern.

Caveats. Inappropriate disclosure of student information often occurs for seemingly appropriate reasons. For example, opening and displaying a grade book during parent-teacher conferences to show a student's progress may also reveal the evaluation results of other children. Such revelations may harm the student involved or other students whose grades were revealed. Teachers and others must plan for such situations, so that they provide needed information while keeping other confidential information secure.

GUIDELINES

A. Maintain a file of current federal and state laws and regulations regarding parent and student rights, and establish procedures for keeping the file current.

B. Prepare and implement clear district-, school-, and classroom-level policies that specify allowable access to student evaluation information. These policies should identify legitimate users and uses (see U2, Defined Users and Uses) and be consistent with applicable laws and the basic principles of fairness and human rights.

C. Establish written policies and procedures for the public display of student evaluation information, including the consent of parents/guardians and, where appropriate, students.

D. Inform students and their parents/guardians about the procedures for exercising their rights to review the student's data, information, and evaluation results (see P5, Rights of Students).

E. Maintain records of access to or release of student evaluation information. For each access or release, records should include the following:

- The name of the person or persons who released and received the information

- The basis for releasing the information
- A description of the information released
- The date the information was released
- Any constraints placed on its use
- Safeguards taken to maintain confidentiality and protect privacy

F. Arrange for the secure storage of evaluation data, results, and reports. Specify procedures, rights, and safeguards (e.g., use of passwords and other security devices) for any electronic storage of student evaluation records that parallel procedures for accessing student evaluation results and information (see A8, Handling Information and Quality Control).

G. Guide the transfer of evaluative information from one school to another using a written policy with stringent provisions to ensure the maintenance of confidentiality.

H. Establish the length of time student evaluation information is to be retained, and policies and procedures for removing and destroying information that is out of date.

COMMON ERRORS

A. Announcing favorable information (e.g., honor roll) publicly without first obtaining student and parent/guardian consent

B. Discussing student evaluation information with persons who have no need or right to know, such as other teachers, a teacher's own family members or neighbors, and other parents or students

C. Granting access to persons of some standing or authority who have no legitimate need to see a student's evaluation information or report

D. Failing to properly archive and secure historical evaluation information

Illustrative Case 1—Description

Mr. Gould, a third-grade teacher, was concerned that his students were not familiar with the multiple-choice format to be used in the upcoming state assessment. He decided to give a practice test to his students one week before the state assessment, so that they would be familiar with this item format, which he rarely used in his classroom assessments. He gave the practice test early in the morning, collected the tests, scored them, and over the lunch period reviewed the class performance. During the afternoon, the class became a bit unruly. To regain control of the class and focus the students on the upcoming state test, he read the student marks out loud to the class by name.

One girl received a very low score. She managed to hide her embarrassment and sense of inferiority for the rest of the school day. However, when she got home, she was very upset, telling her mother that she was "stupid and that all the other kids knew she was stupid."

Illustrative Case 1—Analysis

Mr. Gould inappropriately used test results for class management purposes (see U2, Defined Users and Uses). He failed to maintain confidentiality and showed a lack of respect to his students. No student should be made to feel embarrassed or "stupid" (see P4, Treatment of Students).

Mr. Gould should have provided the marks to the students individually and in a way that protected each student's privacy. Alternatively, he could have gone over the practice test, discussing areas of strength and weakness, giving special attention to items on which the class as a whole performed less well. He also could have provided individual help for the students who did less well (see U7, Follow-Up). Both of these actions would protect the privacy of each student, while providing extra help and attention.

Illustrative Case 2—Description

The parents of George, a student in grade 8, were concerned with their son's progress in mathematics. They decided to hire a tutor through a university education department's school tutoring program. The tutor was a student in pre-service teacher education. Working with the parents, the tutor decided that she needed more information from the school. In particular, she was interested in seeing what George had been studying, what tests had been given, and what kinds of errors he was making. She suggested that she and the parents approach the mathematics teacher together to see what information they could gather.

The school had in place a clear policy regarding the use of student information by parents/guardians and anyone that the parents/guardians designated. Teachers were to supply the information upon request, providing it did not violate the confidentiality and privacy of other students in the class. Consequently, when the parents and tutor approached the math teacher, he was cooperative in providing the information they requested and did so in a manner that protected the identity of the remaining students in his class. He also outlined the material he would be covering during the next term, provided sample worksheets and problem sets, and lent the tutor an extra copy of the teacher's edition of the textbook.

Illustrative Case 2—Analysis

The parents, tutor, and teacher all worked responsibly for the good of the student. The parents and tutor had a clear idea of the information they needed. The school had a policy in place for the release of student information. The teacher was familiar with the policy. Furthermore, with the clear consent of the parents, he anticipated the additional needs of the tutor and volunteered information and materials to facilitate the tutoring (see P1, Service to Students).

Supporting Documentation

American Educational Research Association, American Psychological Association, & National Council on Measurement in Education. (1999). *Standards for educational and psychological testing.* Washington, DC: American Educational Research Association.

American Federation of Teachers, National Council on Measurement in Education, and National Education Association. (1990). *Standards for teacher competence in educational assessment of students.* Washington, DC: National Council on Measurement in Education.

Joint Advisory Committee. (1993). *Principles for fair student assessment practices for education in Canada.* Edmonton, Alberta, Canada: University of Alberta, Centre for Research in Applied Measurement and Evaluation.

Joint Committee on Testing Practices. (1998). *Code of fair testing practices in education.* Washington, DC: American Psychological Association.

Joint Committee on Testing Practices. (1999). *Test takers' rights and responsibilities.* Washington, DC: American Psychological Association.

National Education Association. (1992). *Handbook: Ethical standards for teachers' relations with pupils.* Washington, DC: Author.

Scriven, M. (1991). *Evaluation thesaurus* (4th ed.). Newbury Park, CA: Sage.

P4 Treatment of Students

STANDARD Students should be treated with respect in all aspects of the evaluation process, so that their dignity and opportunities for educational development are enhanced.

Overview

Explanation. Evaluators must recognize and respond to students' personal and instructional needs. When students are treated with respect, they are more likely to receive fair and equitable treatment, regardless of their individual characteristics or their special group status (e.g., age, gender, ability, language, opportunity to learn, race, ethnicity, or special needs; see A3, Context Analysis). Evaluators should develop and maintain rapport, be professional, and follow institutional policies and procedures in evaluating the student. Assessment items and tasks that refer to emotionally charged topics (e.g., serious illness, suicide, death, divorce, loss of employment, natural disasters); offensive topics (e.g., drinking, drug use); and controversial topics (e.g., slavery, gun control, homosexuality) should be avoided unless their use can be clearly linked to the purposes and use of the evaluation.

Rationale. When teachers respect human dignity and have a positive rapport with their students, the students are less likely to be anxious and more likely to feel positive about an evaluation. When an evaluation is conducted in this manner, sensitive to student needs and differences, the findings are more likely to be presented and received as constructive and oriented toward student growth. The morale of students and the credibility of the evaluation process will likely be enhanced. When negative findings and accompanying evidence are presented clearly, objectively, and privately, the student is more likely to judge the process as fair and the evaluator as considerate. Overall, maintaining good interpersonal relations can support the student's sense of worth and strengthen the use of evaluation to serve the student's educational development.

Caveats. Teachers sometimes use evaluation information to maintain discipline, to put students "in their place," or to tease students. Occasionally, disrespect on the part of students prompts a teacher to use evaluation findings to "hit back." Such actions devalue evaluation and should always be avoided.

GUIDELINES

A. Inform students and their parents/guardians about all aspects of the evaluation process. The information to be provided should include the following:
   - The assessment methods and procedures to be used
   - How the results and collected information will be reported and used
   - The process for students and their parents/guardians to appeal an assessment result, grade, or report (see U6, Effective Reporting)

B. Provide evaluation information to all students in a respectful manner, being careful to consider the rights of students and their varying abilities.

C. Use language appropriate to the students' level of understanding and language skills. With students who possess limited English proficiency, this may involve communication in the student's first language, perhaps with assistance from an interpreter.

D. Encourage students to take responsibility for their own learning and for making the evaluation process meaningful for them personally.

E. Provide evidence that inferences based on results obtained from assessment instruments translated into a second language or transferred from another context or performed at another location are valid for the intended purpose (see A1, Validity Orientation).

F. Try to understand the cultural and social values of all students. Avoid topics that may be sensitive for particular groups of students unless their use can be clearly linked to the purpose and use of the evaluation (see U1, Constructive Orientation; U2, Defined Users and Uses).

G. Establish procedures for dealing with students who are not able to respond to an assessment as administered (e.g., those with disabilities or language barriers) or who become ill during the assessment or are otherwise unable to continue.

H. Communicate results and supporting evidence clearly, objectively, privately, and sensitively, so that students see the value of the evaluation findings in relation to the purposes and uses of the evaluation.

I. Monitor the conduct of the evaluation process to determine if it has been conducted fairly and respectfully.

COMMON ERRORS

A. Performing an evaluation quickly in an effort to be efficient
B. Failing to recognize and attend to signs that a student feels a lack of respect or an inability to be heard during the evaluation process
C. Assuming that all students completely understand the instructions for an assessment method
D. Failing to determine and communicate the expected benefits and obligations of the evaluation process
E. Failing to consider and assess the evaluation information carefully and thoroughly, so that accurate and fair results are reported
F. Publicly reporting the evaluation results of individual students without first obtaining consent from the students and their parents/guardians
G. Inappropriately using the evaluation process or findings to control students' nonacademic behavior (see U2, Defined Users and Uses)
H. Prohibiting a student and, where applicable, his or her parents/guardians access to the student's evaluation results (see P3, Access to Evaluation Information)

Illustrative Case 1—Description

When Mr. Lang, a ninth-grade science teacher, returned the results of the Unit 3 test, he told his students that he was delighted with their achievement. He said that they had shown great interest in the topic of insects throughout the unit, studied hard, collected many specimens, and produced exceptionally fine writing and artwork.

Then, without warning or discussion, Mr. Lang named the three students in the class who had received the top scores. All of this was done as a "celebration of learning" activity where all class members were to rejoice in the learning that had taken place and a job well done. However, later, during the same class period, Mr. Lang openly criticized two students whose projects did not meet his standards of quality and whose test scores were well below the class average.

Illustrative Case 1—Analysis

Celebrating learning that has taken place in the classroom is sound educational practice. However, Mr. Lang's celebration was not fully respectful of his students. He failed to consider the feelings of the top three students, who may not have wanted to be singled out for recognition. In addition, students who had worked hard may have felt discouraged that they did not receive individual public recognition. Similarly, Mr. Lang's criticism likely embarrassed and possibly harmed the two lower performing students. His public comments may have reinforced the image that they were poor students and unable to do well on subsequent assignments and tests.

Mr. Lang should have notified his students and their parents/guardians at the beginning of the school year that he planned to celebrate learning and announce the names of students who had performed exceptionally well and asked permission to release their names (see P3, Access to Evaluation Information). At the same time, he should have avoided making negative comments about other students in public. Negative comments are best made privately to the individual student.

Illustrative Case 2—Description

Many new students from homes where Vietnamese was spoken enrolled in Glendale Elementary School during the first two weeks of the term. When the parents registered their children at the school, they were told that as part of state and local requirements, their children would be given an oral English language proficiency test. This test would help determine if they qualified for special English for Speakers of Other Languages (ESOL) services. A teacher trained as a language assessor and bilingual in English and Vietnamese provided this explanation and completed the assessments.

Each student was assessed individually in private. When the teacher went to each classroom to assess a student, she greeted the child in Vietnamese and explained that it was time for the assessment. When they arrived at the testing room, she took time to orient each student to the testing setting, explained the importance of the assessment, and described the procedures to be followed. Following the prescribed procedures, she told the students that they could take as much time as they needed. She followed standardized procedures as she scored the tests and interpreted the results to determine each student's need for special language services.

Illustrative Case 2—Analysis

The teacher's caring, thorough, and respectful manner enhanced the testing conditions, leading to more reliable and valid test results (see A1, Validity Orientation; A6, Reliable Information). She established rapport with each student, made students comfortable by greeting them in their first language, and explained the expectations and purposes of the assessment. Her bilingual skills made the students feel more at ease, which helped secure their cooperation and allowed them to focus on doing their best.

Supporting Documentation

American Educational Research Association, American Psychological Association, & National Council on Measurement in Education. (1999). *Standards for educational and psychological testing.* Washington, DC: American Educational Research Association.

Cangelosi, J. S. (2000). *Assessment strategies of monitoring student learning.* New York: Longman.

Joint Advisory Committee. (1993). *Principles for fair student assessment practices for education in Canada.* Edmonton, Alberta, Canada: University of Alberta, Centre for Research in Applied Measurement and Evaluation.

Joint Committee on Testing Practices. (1998). *Code of fair testing practices in education.* Washington, DC: American Psychological Association.

Joint Committee on Testing Practices. (1999). *Test takers' rights and responsibilities.* Washington, DC: American Psychological Association.

National Education Association. (1992). *Handbook: Ethical standards for teachers' relations with pupils.* Washington, DC: Author.

U.S. Department of Education, Office for Civil Rights. (2000). *The use of tests as part of high-stakes decision-making for students: A resource guide for educators and policy-makers.* Washington, DC: Author. Retrieved May 17, 2002, from http://www.ed.gov/offices/OCR/testing/.

van der Vijer, F. J. R., & Hambleton, R. K. (1996). Translating tests: Some practical guidelines. *European Psychologist, 1,* 89-99.

P5 Rights of Students

STANDARD Evaluations of students should be consistent with applicable laws and basic principles of fairness and human rights, so that students' rights and welfare are protected.

Overview

Explanation. Students being evaluated have specific rights. Some of these rights are based in law and school policy (see P3, Access to Evaluation Information), whereas others are based on accepted ethical practice, common sense, and courtesy. Legal provisions include those that deal with confidentiality of information, privacy, health, and safety protections. For specialized testing performed by counselors and school psychologists, legal provisions require consent by the students or, where applicable, their parents/guardians. Ethical, common sense, and courtesy considerations include such aspects as avoiding harmful or uncomfortable experiences, and taking account of the ages, abilities, and special needs of the students being assessed.

Rationale. Evaluators should be knowledgeable about and adhere to both legal and human rights requirements in their evaluations. Those who are poorly informed about the legal and personal rights of students and others affected by the evaluation may unwittingly ignore or abuse these rights, thereby harming the students. Evaluators who knowingly or unknowingly violate a student's legal and ethical rights may be subject to legal actions and/or professional sanction. Failure to respect the rights of students and to show courtesy may deny some students the opportunity to participate and succeed in the education to which they are entitled.

Caveats. The authority that teachers have over students, the closed nature of the classroom, and the close relationship between teachers and their students creates an environment where inappropriate handling of evaluation information by teachers may occur (e.g., sharing of information that is privileged). Teachers must be alert to what they say and do to guard against infringing on students' rights. Students, for example, often want to compare their own performance on assessments against that of their friends. If the teacher discloses such information to a student's friend, then the rights of the student have been violated.

GUIDELINES

A. Learn what rights students derive from the law and from school policy, and conduct student evaluations that conform to these rights.

B. Inform students and their parents/guardians of their rights in an evaluation (see P3, Access to Evaluation Information).

C. Communicate evaluation policies and information to students and their parents/guardians in language that is understandable to them. Elements to consider include the following:
   - Purposes of student evaluation
   - Uses to which evaluation information will be put
   - Types of assessments to be used
   - Conditions under which alternative assessments will be provided
   - Benefits and consequences of evaluations
   - Timing of reports and parent-teacher conferences
   - Procedures to appeal the results of a report
   - Evaluation situations for which written consent or permission may be requested

D. Consider the backgrounds and learning experiences of the students when developing or selecting assessment methods and interpreting assessment results. Some factors to consider are age, ability, gender, language, opportunity to learn, socioeconomic background, and, if present, learning disability.

E. Inform students and parents/guardians of the implications of evaluation findings.

F. Where needed, secure a signed parent's/guardian's permission form (see P3, Access to Evaluation Information).

COMMON ERRORS

A. Failing to recognize the importance of knowing and protecting students' rights

B. Failing to ensure that students and parents/guardians understand the evaluation findings when their first language is not the dominant language used in the school

C. Failing to implement appropriate evaluation accommodations for students with disabilities (see P4, Treatment of Students)
D. Divulging privileged evaluation information without obtaining proper permission to do so (see U2, Defined Users and Uses)

Illustrative Case 1—Description

Ms. Myers was implementing the new districtwide, standards-based mathematics curriculum in her eighth-grade classroom. The results from tests given at specific intervals during the year will form the basis for deciding whether students are promoted to ninth grade. Ms. Myers was concerned about Tom, a bright student who is dyslexic. His Individual Educational Program (IEP) was explicit about his need for accommodations, but less instructive about specific methodology to implement the accommodations. With the support of the district curriculum coordinator, Ms. Myers contacted the textbook publisher and found that the text, student workbooks, and tests were available on both tape and CD-ROM. She talked with Tom's parents and found that the digital material could be accessed through the adaptive technology devices on Tom's computer. Consequently, Tom used both the tape and digital materials.

Illustrative Case 1—Analysis

Ms. Myers and school personnel understood their responsibilities to protect Tom's right to an appropriate education. As is sometimes the case, the IEP detailed the student's disability but provided little specificity as to how a teacher could meet his needs. Ms. Myers accepted her responsibility and worked with the curriculum coordinator and Tom's parents. Communication was open, but not beyond the circle of those who had a right to know. Tom's right to take the same test with appropriate accommodation, not an alternative assessment, was respected. Protecting Tom's rights resulted in a greater likelihood that a fair and sound evaluation would be made and that the evaluation would be useful to him.

Illustrative Case 2—Description

Ms. Martin, with the consent of her students and their parents/guardians, always exhibits the best work of her fifth-grade students on the wall outside her room. Sometimes, she displays their artwork, but more often she presents their creative writing. She works to ensure that no student is left out more than twice in a row. Her students like and trust her, and they are inclined to tell her things in their stories that are important to them. Sometimes, students play out their fears in their stories, particularly in stories based on fairy tales and myths.

Glen had written a particularly fierce story that was the best narrative he had done that year. He had worked on the sentence structure, spelling, and vibrant choice of words. Ms. Martin wanted to display the story, but Glen said that he did not want his story displayed. Ms. Martin respected Glen's wishes and did not exhibit his story, thinking that perhaps he was telling her something private in the guise of a tale. In any case, it was his right to keep his writing to himself and to share it only with Ms. Martin.

Illustrative Case 2—Analysis

Ms. Martin respected her students' rights to their own work. Why Glen preferred not to have his story made public is irrelevant. Ms. Martin's students are required to produce work for her when she asks for it. They are not, however, required to have their work published to a wider audience unless they give their permission. It was Glen's right to keep his writing to himself and to share it only with his teacher. Consequently, access to evaluation information in Ms. Martin's class is controlled and protected.

Supporting Documentation

American Educational Research Association, American Psychological Association, & National Council on Measurement in Education. (1999). *Standards for educational and psychological testing.* Washington, DC: American Educational Research Association.

American Federation of Teachers, National Council on Measurement in Education, & National Education Association. (1990). *Standards for teacher competence in educational assessment of students.* Washington, DC: National Council on Measurement in Education.

Joint Advisory Committee. (1993). *Principles for fair student assessment practices for education in Canada.* Edmonton, Alberta, Canada: University of Alberta, Centre for Research in Applied Measurement and Evaluation.

Joint Committee on Testing Practices. (1998). *Code of fair testing practices in education.* Washington, DC: American Psychological Association.

Joint Committee on Testing Practices. (1999). *Test takers' rights and responsibilities.* Washington, DC: American Psychological Association.

National Education Association. (1992). *Handbook: Ethical standards for teachers' relations with pupils.* Washington, DC: Author.

U.S. Department of Education, Office for Civil Rights. (2000). *The use of tests as part of high-stakes decision-making for students: A resource guide for educators and policy-makers.* Washington, DC: Author. Retrieved May 17, 2002, from http://www.ed.gov/offices/OCR/testing/.

P6 Balanced Evaluation

STANDARD Evaluations of students should provide information that identifies both strengths and weaknesses, so that strengths can be built upon and problem areas addressed.

Overview

Explanation. Knowledge of both strengths and weaknesses is required for balanced instructional planning. A balanced evaluation helps to reduce errors and stimulates and reinforces improved performance. Knowledge of strengths (e.g., mastery of information or skills, positive aptitude) provides building blocks for planning and reinforcing student learning. Knowledge of student weaknesses (e.g., student misconceptions, gaps in knowledge, conditions impeding learning) enables problem areas to be addressed and obstacles to be overcome or circumvented.

Identification of strengths and weaknesses requires credible frames of reference. Typical frames of reference include the following:

- Performance in relation to specified standards
- Performance in relation to peers
- Performance in relation to aptitude or expected growth
- Performance in terms of the amount of improvement
- Performance in terms of the amount learned

These frames of reference help ensure that findings will be understood, believed, and used by the student or others who must act on the information. If, for example, a decision is to be made about whether a student is ready to move on to the next unit in an instructional sequence, interpretations based on prespecified standards would be appropriate.

Rationale. Evaluations of students should help them develop to their fullest potential. Failure to address either strengths or weaknesses results in biases. These biases reduce validity (see A1, Validity Orientation) and utility (see U2, Defined Users and Uses) of evaluation information.

Caveats. Balancing an evaluation does not mean generating equal numbers of strengths and weaknesses. It means being thorough and fair in evaluating both.

GUIDELINES

A. Ensure that the assessment procedures allow comprehensive and consistent indications of the strengths and weaknesses of the students being evaluated. Avoid duplicating information already collected or available.
B. Inform students about what will be assessed, how the evaluation information will be used to identify strengths and weaknesses, and how the results will be used to design appropriate follow-up actions (see U7, Follow-Up).
C. Describe and justify the basis for interpretation of assessment information and results.
D. To the extent possible, engage students in the evaluation process to facilitate their understanding of the results and their involvement in follow-up actions (see U7, Follow-Up).
E. Solicit comments about the thoroughness and fairness of the evaluation process from other teachers, school officials, students, parents/guardians, and other stakeholders (see P4, Treatment of Students).

COMMON ERRORS

A. Manipulating the evaluation of strengths and weaknesses or discontinuing an evaluation that may prove embarrassing to please individual(s) with a vested interest
B. Reporting only positive findings and ignoring negative findings or reporting only negative findings and ignoring positive findings
C. Failing to consider alternative perspectives that might change the interpretation of an evaluation result

Illustrative Case 1—Description

Concerned with low standardized test performance, many students and parents/guardians in the Oakmont school district appeared to be developing a negative attitude toward Grandview Elementary School. To counteract this attitude, administrators decided that the "positive" should be emphasized in learning, and that what was learned by each student should be "celebrated." Neither teachers nor parents/guardians of the students were consulted in making this decision.

At the beginning of the year, all teachers received a memo directing them to develop anecdotal report cards and base their judgments on "non-test" data. They were to describe the performances of each student in positive terms so that "a student's learning could be celebrated." Numerical grade information was not to be reported.

Many parents/guardians attended the parent-teacher conferences held during the year. Most expressed displeasure with their child's report cards. Two common questions were asked: (1) You have told me what my child can do, but what is he/she having trouble with? (2) You have told me what my child can do, but how does he/she compare with other students in the class? Parents pointed out that without this knowledge, they would not be able to help their children. Teachers, too, indicated that they had difficulty with this evaluation system, commenting that they found it time-consuming, awkward, problematic to ignore test findings, and difficult to craft positive statements to reflect apparent weaknesses.

In light of parent/guardian questions and teachers' comments, the evaluation procedure was changed the following year to allow the identification of both strengths and weaknesses. Developed by a committee representing the administration, teachers, and parents, the revised evaluation system was much more acceptable to the parents and the teachers than the system it replaced.

Illustrative Case 1—Analysis

Clearly, many parents and teachers thought the evaluations conducted by the teachers lacked balance. Even when the primary purpose of an evaluation is to determine what students can do, it is essential to identify what students cannot do as well. The situation at Grandview Elementary School arose from the administration's unilateral decision. Administrators failed to solicit comments, reactions, and advice from teachers or parents/guardians, two major users of student evaluation information (see P1, Service to Students). Balanced information necessary to guide follow-up actions was not available. Consequently, the needs of students, parents/guardians, and teachers were not fully met.

On a constructive note, administrators were responsive to the reactions of parents/guardians and teachers, and acted promptly to discontinue the "positive" evaluation system. Representatives of the administration then worked with teachers and parents/guardians to design a replacement that allowed the identification of both strengths and weaknesses.

Supporting Documentation

Airasian, P. W. (1997). *Classroom assessment* (3rd edition). New York: McGraw-Hill.

Linn, R. L., & Gronlund, N. E. (2000). *Measurement and assessment in teaching* (8th edition). Upper Saddle River, NJ: Prentice Hall.

Joint Advisory Committee. (1993). *Principles for fair student assessment practices for education in Canada.* Edmonton, Alberta, Canada: University of Alberta, Centre for Research in Applied Measurement and Evaluation.

Stiggins, R. J. (1997). *Student-centered classroom assessment.* Upper Saddle River, NJ: Prentice Hall.

P7 Conflict of Interest

STANDARD Conflicts of interest should be avoided, but if present should be dealt with openly and honestly, so that they do not compromise evaluation processes and results.

Overview

Explanation. Conflicts of interest arise when the goals and biases of evaluators inappropriately influence a judgment or decision. Conflicts of interest can intrude at several points in the student evaluation process, including planning the evaluation design, collecting data, analyzing and interpreting data, and reporting evaluation findings to students and their parents/guardians.

Sources of conflict of interest are many and varied. They often occur when a teacher's livelihood, reputation, or career advancement may be affected by student evaluation results. By evaluating a student more positively than warranted by evidence, a teacher might improve his or her own standing with a superior (e.g., when a teacher is evaluating the child of a supervising administrator). A teacher also might bias evaluation results when a student could be excluded from extracurricular activities due to poor academic performance (e.g., when a teacher is an athletic coach for the student). Other conflicts may arise from differing philosophies of education, political preferences, cultural backgrounds, and moral codes (see U5, Explicit Values).

Rationale. Conflicts of interest can undermine a student evaluation to the point that the integrity of the judgments made is suspect. Decisions about students are questionable if the belief exists that the evaluations of any students were influenced by personal self-interest. Eliminating or openly addressing these conflicts when elimination is not feasible helps to ensure fair, acceptable, and usable evaluations.

Caveats. Conflicts of interest can have such a powerful and negative influence on evaluations and those affected that even the appearance of impropriety can reduce the intended impact of an evaluation. Therefore, whether conflicts of interest are real or merely perceived, teachers should pay close attention to the potential for them when planning an evaluation and when scoring, interpreting, reporting, and using evaluation results.

GUIDELINES

A. Encourage cooperative development of evaluation designs, so that the possibility of conflicts of interest is reduced.
B. Identify common sources of conflicts of interest in written evaluation policies and guidelines.
C. Ensure that all those who might be involved in a conflict of interest situation know about the potential for a conflict. Define in writing the procedures to be followed if it is impossible to eliminate the potential for conflict.
D. Control conflicts of interest at every level of an evaluation. For example, use an assessment method that can be objectively scored, create clear scoring rubrics and model answers for subjectively scored assessments, have at least a sample of subjectively scored assessments checked by a disinterested third party, and compare the results from different assessment methods.
E. Ensure the security of all assessment instruments and scores that could become part of a conflict-of-interest situation (see A8, Handling Information and Quality Control).

COMMON ERRORS

A. Failing to remove or control the potential for conflict (e.g., making the evaluation the sole responsibility of a teacher when the potential for conflict is known)
B. Failing to provide an appeal process to resolve a conflict-of-interest situation
C. Having judges in an appeal hearing who are involved in the conflict of interest being heard.
D. Ignoring conflict-of-interest situations because reporting them requires additional effort or may result in controversy and disputes.

Illustrative Case 1—Description

Ms. Hanson has applied for the district's language arts curriculum specialist position, and the superintendent will make the decision. She has not told anyone at her school about her application for the position, because she wishes to avoid embarrassment in case she does not get the job. The superintendent's son is in her English class, and she just gave the major exam for the third reporting period. Like all of her tests, it was an essay exam.

Ms. Hanson holistically graded the student papers over the weekend. Being sensitive to her conflict-of-interest situation, she was careful not to look at the students' names at the top of their papers. Despite her care, there were two papers she thought might have been written by the superintendent's son. She graded the tests and noticed, as she put the grades in her grade book, that the superintendent's son, who is generally a B student, got an A.

Illustrative Case 1—Analysis

Although the grade received by the superintendent's son might not have had any effect on the decision regarding the appointment of the new language arts specialist, Ms. Hanson should have done more to control the potential conflict of interest she has recognized. In addition to notifying her immediate supervisor or department head, she could have developed model answers and procedures to make the essay scoring process more objective. She could also have asked another teacher who was not aware of her conflict-of-interest situation to grade the superintendent's son's paper together with some other students' papers. The inclusion of other students' papers would allow a comparison between the two teachers' scoring. If there was a high degree of agreement in the way both teachers scored the essays, this would help rule out conflict of interest as the reason for the high grade of the superintendent's son. If the agreement was low, then the teachers should discuss the discrepancies between the two sets of marks. Once consensus is reached, each teacher should re-mark the papers.

Illustrative Case 2—Description

The school board in a large suburban district requires that a standardized achievement battery be administered to all middle school students at the end of the school year. This action was taken in response to the perception that student performance in the district was too low. If this low performance is confirmed, school board members have indicated that they would consider instituting an annual end-of-year testing program, with the results reported to the public.

In one school, the principal called a meeting well in advance of the test date to advise her teachers about the upcoming testing. She emphasized the importance of student performance on the test, because the district planned to publish reports of the performance on each subject at each grade level for each school. The principal encouraged the teachers to do whatever they could to ensure student success. She closed the meeting by saying that copies of the tests were available in a file in the teachers' lounge, and that teachers might want "to take a look" at them so they will know how to prepare students for the test.

Two grade 7 teachers responded differently to the principal's demand for high performance. Ms. Arnett had a background in assessment and was very secure in her job. She did not look at the tests, but provided her students with some experience in answering questions by filling in bubbles on a timed test of the material she was teaching at the time. Mr. Langer, less secure in his job, believed that tests define specific things his students should know, and it just "makes sense" to write down the specific concepts and facts on the test and teach them to all his students. Consequently, he looked at the tests, so that he knew what to teach his students. He did not understand that the standardized test would measure only a small sample of the desired student outcomes for grade 7.

The test results for the school were slightly above the average for the district, an outcome consistent with the type of community the school serves. The seventh-grade scores were about average, with Mr. Langer's class average about one standard deviation higher than Ms. Arnett's class average. The school received no reprimand from the school board and no bad press. The principal knew what had happened and said nothing about the differences between Mr. Langer's class and Ms. Arnett's class. However, she did make a positive note in Mr. Langer's confidential file and a corresponding negative note in Ms. Arnett's. Parents who come to look at the test scores of Ms. Arnett's students were somewhat troubled to see that their children did not do as well as the district average nor as well as the students in Mr. Langer's class. Parents of Mr. Langer's students, on the other hand, were generally pleased.

Illustrative Case 2—Analysis

There are two potential sources of conflict of interest here. Teachers who administer the tests will be evaluated positively or negatively based on the scores of their students. The schools, and therefore the school administrators, face the same situation. Hence, as indicated by the principal, it is in the interest of all parties that students score well on these tests.

This poses an ethical dilemma. Although the expectation is that teachers will respond in the same way to the presence of an external examination, the two teachers in this case responded differently. To the extent that these different responses produced both short- and longer-term differences in performance, an ethical issue arises. This could have been avoided if the school district had advised teachers on what was expected of them in preparing the students both for the test and for the next grade.

The district policy of making fair, high-stakes decisions from valid test scores is ethically incompatible with the practice of allowing teachers and principals to examine the tests well before they are administered. The district should find a way to keep the tests secure and ensure that there is a close alignment between the curriculum and what the tests measure, so that resulting evaluation reports, from the individual student level to the superintendent level, reflect pertinent and valid information.

Supporting Documentation

Airasian, P. W. (1997). *Classroom assessment* (3rd edition). New York: McGraw-Hill.

Joint Advisory Committee. (1993). *Principles for fair student assessment practices for education in Canada*. Edmonton, Alberta, Canada: University of Alberta, Centre for Research in Applied Measurement and Evaluation.

Linn, R. L., & Gronlund, N. E. (2000). *Measurement and assessment in teaching* (8th edition). Upper Saddle River, NJ: Prentice Hall.

U UTILITY STANDARDS

Summary of the Standards

U Utility Standards The utility standards help ensure that student evaluations are useful. Useful student evaluations are informative, timely, and influential. Standards that support usefulness are as follows:

U1 Constructive Orientation Student evaluations should be constructive, so that they result in educational decisions that are in the best interest of the student.

U2 Defined Users and Uses The users and uses of a student evaluation should be specified, so that evaluation appropriately contributes to student learning and development.

U3 Information Scope The information collected for student evaluations should be carefully focused and sufficiently comprehensive, so that evaluation questions can be fully answered and the needs of students addressed.

U4 Evaluator Qualifications Teachers and others who evaluate students should have the necessary knowledge and skills, so that evaluations are carried out competently and the results can be used with confidence.

U5 Explicit Values In planning and conducting student evaluations, teachers and others who evaluate students should identify and justify the values used to judge student performance, so that the bases for the evaluations are clear and defensible.

U6 Effective Reporting Student evaluation reports should be clear, timely, accurate, and relevant, so that they are useful to students, their parents/guardians, and other legitimate users.

U7 Follow-Up Student evaluations should include procedures for follow-up, so that students, parents/guardians, and other legitimate users can understand the information and take appropriate follow-up actions.

U1 Constructive Orientation

STANDARD Student evaluations should be constructive, so that they result in educational decisions that are in the best interest of the student.

Overview

Explanation. Student evaluations should be planned and implemented, so that results can be used to increase the likelihood that students will benefit. In a constructive evaluation environment, all stakeholders can benefit from information about the students' strengths and weaknesses. Information about both these areas, reported in a constructive manner, enables students to direct their energies effectively, provides parents/guardians with information they can use to assist their children, and helps educators plan and implement appropriate opportunities to learn.

Rationale. Constructive evaluations encourage and support student development and learning. To encourage beneficial aspects and avoid detrimental aspects of student evaluations, evaluators should employ practices that provide useful information about student knowledge, skills, attitudes, and behavior. With this information, school personnel are better able to encourage student growth and learning and provide them with superior, pertinent services.

Caveats. Evaluations that are used to control or intimidate students or that emphasize negative results discourage students and may inhibit their learning. Evaluations that identify weaknesses but do not assist in correcting deficiencies contribute little to the students, their parents/guardians, or other legitimate users.

GUIDELINES

A. Ensure that students, their parents/guardians, teachers, and other legitimate users understand the purposes and uses of the evaluations (see U2, Defined Users and Uses).
B. Provide timely evaluation feedback and decisions to all stakeholders (see U6, Effective Reporting).
C. Discuss evaluation results and findings in a positive way, avoiding an adversarial approach and emphasizing appropriate support for the growth of the student.
D. Ensure that evaluative information is used in intended ways and that follow-up actions are relevant and meaningful (see U7, Follow-Up).

COMMON ERRORS

A. Assuming that the purposes of the evaluation process are inherently self-explanatory, acceptable to all parties, and beneficial to the student
B. Failing to recognize and respond to both strengths and weaknesses of a student's performance
C. Withholding evaluative information relevant to the decisions to be made, presuming that the information withheld would not be in the student's best interests
D. Using student evaluations as a method for maintaining discipline or as a form of punishment.

Illustrative Case 1—Description

Ms. Otani, an elementary school counselor, arranged a final conference for the parents of a grade 1 student diagnosed with a major learning disability. The diagnosis was based on results from a battery of tests she had administered and scored and reports from a reading specialist, audiologist, and neurologist. Ms. Otani arranged the conference with the parents so that these three professionals, the student's teacher, and the principal could attend the meeting. She also advised the parents, who were very concerned and willing to do whatever was necessary for their child, that they could have someone accompany them to the meeting if they wished. The parents said that Ms. Otani had approached them before the testing to discuss their child's performance, the reasons for the testing, and the need for their consent. They chose to attend the meeting without additional support, indicating to Ms. Otani that they had confidence in her and what she was doing.

During the meeting, the teacher described how she had arrived at the decision to refer the child to the counselor for testing. Then, beginning with the counselor, the specialists presented brief, non-technical reports of their test results. The parents, teacher, and principal were encouraged to ask questions at any point. Particular attention was given to follow-up actions, which involved transferring the student to another school that was better able to meet her needs. At the completion of the meeting, the parents were asked if they understood all that had been discussed, and they again were given an opportunity to ask questions and seek advice.

Following the meeting, with parental approval, Ms. Otani and the principal worked with the parents to arrange a transfer to the other school and for bus transportation to be provided by the district. Ms. Otani also assured the parents that they could contact her in the future should they have any further questions.

Illustrative Case 1—Analysis

Ms. Otani was prepared to conduct a meaningful conference. She focused on the need to help the student and her parents. She maintained contact with the parents during the testing, anticipated the parents' information needs, and arranged a constructive meeting with the evaluation team. Ms. Otani ensured as best she could that the parents understood the evaluative information they had been provided. She offered multiple opportunities for the parents and others to ask questions. Together with the principal, Ms. Otani worked to ensure that follow-up actions were properly implemented.

Illustrative Case 2—Description

Tanya, an elementary student, brought home a story that she had written in response to the following assignment: Write a story about someone or something about which you care deeply. The assignment was intended to assess the students' writing ability after a period of writing instruction and to identify strengths and weaknesses.

As Tanya's parents read the story, they found a touching retelling of an event that had recently happened in their family. Several weeks earlier, they had given Tanya a kitten for her birthday. Unfortunately, Tanya's sister was allergic to the kitten, and it had to be returned to its original owner. Understandably, Tanya was upset. All of this was retold in the story. The story was not sophisticated in language or syntax, but it did detail events in order and clearly depicted the strong emotions that surrounded the return of the kitten.

Tanya used three-quarters of the page to tell her story. In the space left at the bottom, the parents were surprised to see the grade of F. They asked Tanya if she knew why she had received that grade. Tanya said that the teacher had told her she was to fill the page with writing. Tanya then placed the paper on the kitchen table and said, "I will never be good at writing! I can't do it right!"

Illustrative Case 2—Analysis

The main purpose of this writing assessment was to determine each student's current level of writing, so that information would be available to guide future instruction and help students grow. However, the teacher's scoring of Tanya had little to do with writing proficiency, and more to do with following the teacher's directions. More important, Tanya received no feedback about her writing proficiency. The inference that the child made based on the grade she received was that she would never be a good writer.

Sound assessments can be achieved only if direct, relevant feedback is given on the aspects being assessed. The teacher should have commented on the feelings expressed by the student in her writing (see P4, Treatment of Students), pointing out both the strengths and weaknesses of the story. By doing so, she may have avoided the negative feelings of the student and her parents.

Supporting Documentation

Airasian, P. W. (1997). *Classroom assessment* (3rd edition). New York: McGraw-Hill.

Cangelosi, J. S. (2000). *Assessment strategies for monitoring student learning.* New York: Addison Wesley Longman.

Linn, R. L., & Gronlund, N. E. (2000). *Measurement and assessment in teaching.* Upper Saddle River, NJ: Prentice Hall.

Stiggins, R. J. (1997). *Student-centered classroom assessment* (2nd edition). Upper Saddle River, NJ: Prentice Hall.

Thorndike, R. M. (1997). *Measurement and evaluation in psychology and education.* Upper Saddle River, NJ: Merrill.

U.S. Department of Education, Office for Civil Rights. (2000). *The use of tests as part of high-stakes decision-making for students: A resource guide for educators and policy-makers.* Washington, DC: Author. Retrieved May 17, 2002, from http://www.ed.gov/offices/OCR/testing/.

Wiggins, G. P. (1993). *Assessing student performance: Exploring the purpose and limits of testing.* San Francisco: Jossey-Bass.

U2 Defined Users and Uses

STANDARD The users and uses of a student evaluation should be specified, so that evaluation appropriately contributes to student learning and development.

Overview

Explanation. There are many potential users and uses of student evaluation information and results. To ensure that evaluation information will be useful, the users and uses of the findings should be specified. Students need information about their strengths and weaknesses in order to focus their efforts, seek help when needed, maintain faith in their ability to learn, and make decisions about course selection or what to do after high school graduation. Teachers need information to determine student needs, guide student learning, evaluate the impact of their instruction, assign grades, and maintain student confidence.

Parents/guardians of young students use evaluative information almost daily to offer encouragement at home and collaborate productively with their children's teachers. Parents/guardians of older students need this information to help their children select courses and evaluate their options after high school graduation. Principals, department chairs, and curriculum directors need information to develop or modify curricula, allocate resources, and identify student scholarship winners. Special teachers, counselors, and psychologists need information to help identify students with learning disabilities and to develop appropriate educational programs for these students. All these users count on day-to-day classroom assessments when making their decisions and judgments.

Rationale. Student evaluations should be guided by the intended use of the evaluation information. This requires that users be identified and their needs determined during the evaluation planning process. This identification helps ensure that an evaluation is targeted properly and produces useful information. It also safeguards against misuse of evaluation information by limiting access to predetermined purposes and predetermined users.

Caveats. Evaluation information can be used to make formal, high-stakes decisions in situations where students' life choices will be affected or where resources will be allocated and accountability examined. Evaluation information can be used to make informal, low-stakes decisions in day-to-day classroom teaching. In all cases, the student should have a central, active role in the evaluation process and not be treated merely as an object of evaluation. A student's understanding of how the information is to be used is likely to affect the reliability and trustworthiness of the evaluation (see A1, Validity Orientation; A6, Reliable Information).

Student evaluation information applied inappropriately or for other than its intended use may be damaging. As a result, students may come to distrust the evaluation system. They may withhold information, believing that it will be misused, serve no legitimate purpose, or be used to their detriment.

GUIDELINES

A. Include students, their parents/guardians, and other potential users as appropriate when determining the purpose(s) and procedures of an evaluation, and check their level of understanding (see P1, Service to Students).

B. Develop a balanced and integrated evaluation system that avoids duplication while providing information relevant to the needs of users (see P6, Balanced Evaluation).

C. Determine which users are entitled to see what information and enforce these restrictions (see P3, Access to Evaluation Information).

D. Ensure accurate and timely reporting of evaluation information relevant to each user (see U6, Effective Reporting).

E. Monitor the evaluation process to ensure that the evaluation information is actually being used in the ways intended.

COMMON ERRORS

A. Assuming that all users have identical or similar needs that will be met by the same type of student evaluation information

B. Attending primarily to the information needs of the politically important (e.g., policymakers) and ignoring the needs of classroom-level users such as students, parents/guardians, and teachers (see F2, Political Viability)

C. Conducting assessments as a matter of habit or tradition rather than to help make decisions about students or instructional practice

D. Using assessment methods for purposes for which they were not intended

Illustrative Case 1—Description

Satisfactory completion of a university-level introductory chemistry course was required for admission into professional programs in medicine and dentistry. The university instructors designed their tests in this course to distinguish the more able students from the less able students.

Whereas class instruction and laboratory work focused on the fundamentals of chemistry, the tests emphasized extended knowledge and applications. These tests were administrated with a strict time limit, so that only the best prepared and fastest problem solvers completed them. Some knowledgeable students sought help from tutors or upper-level chemistry majors who had taken the course before. Others used informal "test banks" found on campus to better prepare themselves for these high-stakes exams.

During the first year of testing, approximately one-third of the students dropped the course after the first test, and fewer than 15 percent received an A or B grade. The chemistry instructors were satisfied that their evaluation system was rigorous and on target. Meanwhile, officials in the professional health schools complained that many of the A students they admitted were ill prepared in the fundamentals of chemistry. As a result, these officials threatened to admit highly able students directly from high school and to teach their own introductory chemistry course to these new students.

Illustrative Case 1—Analysis

The chemistry instructors were using assessments that did not address the most important evaluation question that the students and admission officers in the professional health schools needed answered: Which students have mastered the fundamentals of chemistry that are taught in the introductory chemistry course? By testing objectives different from the instructional objectives, the instructors encouraged their students to ignore primary course content in order to achieve high scores on the tests. In addition, this evaluation system led to an adversarial relationship between the chemistry department and the professional health schools that relied upon the department to prepare students for the health sciences.

To correct this situation, a course committee with members from both the chemistry department and the professional health schools should be established. The members of this committee would be responsible for reaching a common understanding about what should be taught, and how the students should be evaluated. By doing so, the evaluation results will be more meaningful and useful to the students and the instructors in the professional health schools.

Illustrative Case 2—Description

The teachers in a junior high school English department have developed a new program designed to create proficient writers. The teachers began by developing a clear vision of what good writers know and can produce. They devised clear and appropriate scoring rubrics for evaluating several different kinds of student writing and a training process to train teachers and students how to use them.

At the start of the school year, the teachers inform their students that they want to establish a baseline for writing proficiency, so they can study student growth during the year. They ask their students to write a narrative essay, a persuasive essay, and a poem. These are placed in the students' writing portfolios for later marking. As instruction continues, the teachers have the students analyze writing samples of varying quality to discover the keys to good writing. Working with their teachers, the students create descriptions of poor, midrange, and outstanding writing. Then they evaluate one of their own unmarked pieces from their portfolio to determine where it falls on the continuum of quality. The results are clear. Students now have a sense of their writing strengths and weaknesses at the beginning of the year.

As the school year passes, students build a portfolio of writing samples, each evaluated using the same set of performance criteria used for the first pieces. At midyear, teachers have each student create a new writing sample and evaluate it. They then retrieve another of their writing samples from the beginning of the year, evaluate it, and write a commentary on the differences between the two pieces. The differences are decisive, and the students are impressed with the improvements they have made. The writing portfolios are shared with the students' parents/guardians at student-led conferences to provide concrete examples of the quality of their children's writing and what they can work on at home.

Illustrative Case 2—Analysis

The student evaluation system implemented by the junior high English teachers is closely aligned with the curriculum and instruction provided to the students. The evaluation system yields information about how well the students can write and the progress they are making. The students, aware of their own improvements over time, are motivated to keep trying to improve. The evaluation system fosters growth in the students, while at the same time meeting the needs for evaluation information for mid- and end-of-year reporting.

Supporting Documentation

Airasian, P. W. (1997). *Classroom assessment* (3rd edition). New York: McGraw-Hill.

Cangelosi, J. S. (2000). *Assessment strategies for monitoring student learning.* New York: Addison Wesley Longman.

Linn, R. L., & Gronlund, N. E. (2000). *Measurement and assessment in teaching.* Upper Saddle River, NJ: Prentice Hall.

Stiggins, R. J. (1997). *Student-centered classroom assessment* (2nd edition). Upper Saddle River, NJ: Prentice Hall.

U.S. Department of Education, Office for Civil Rights. (2000). *The use of tests as part of high-stakes decision-making for students: A resource guide for educators and policy-makers.* Washington, DC: Author. Retrieved May 17, 2002, from http://www.ed.gov/offices/OCR/testing/.

U3 Information Scope

STANDARD The information collected for student evaluations should be carefully focused and sufficiently comprehensive, so that evaluation questions can be fully answered and the needs of students addressed.

Overview

Explanation. The information collected in a student evaluation should target the identified evaluation question or need (see U2, Defined Users and Uses). The data and information collected should be relevant to the identified purposes and sufficiently comprehensive to support decisions that need to be made or the actions to be taken.

When determining how comprehensive the data must be, consideration should be given to the consequences of decisions and actions undertaken based on the information from the evaluation (see U7, Follow-Up). For example, course grades are high-stakes evaluation decisions with substantial consequences for students. High-stakes decisions typically require a large amount of information that is broad in scope and gathered over a substantial time span. Low-stakes decisions, such as those made from observations of students during a single class or evaluations of daily homework, typically require a smaller and narrower amount of information gathered in a brief span of time.

Rationale. Prescribing the scope of needed information helps to ensure that student evaluations are sufficiently relevant and comprehensive to support the decisions to be made. If the scope is too narrow, insufficient information will be available to make a meaningful decision. If the scope is too broad, instructional time and student effort will be wasted gathering information that is not needed for the decision, and inappropriate data may be incorporated into the decision-making process, producing invalid decisions.

Caveats. Evaluators should not determine the information scope by limiting the evaluations to information that has been typically collected in the past, can be collected using comfortable or familiar approaches, or is easy to collect. Care must also be taken to ensure that mandated standardized assessment programs do not drive practice. Allowing mandated standardized testing to determine the evaluation scope tends to narrow the evaluation focus. This, in turn, tends to narrow the curriculum to the detriment of student learning.

GUIDELINES

A. Determine the purpose(s) to be served by the evaluation (see P1, Service to Students).
B. Develop a framework or structure (e.g., outline) to identify issues/questions that address the stated purpose(s).
C. Develop an evaluation plan that will produce necessary data and information to address the purpose(s) of the evaluation (see U2, Defined Users and Uses).
D. Develop assessment procedures and items to gain the information identified in the evaluation plan.
E. Verify that the assessment instruments and methods will provide the needed data and information but do not include extraneous items and procedures.
F. Use a variety of evaluation methods to ensure comprehensive and consistent indications of student performance.
G. Inform students and, where needed, other stakeholders of the assessment methods to be used and their relationship to the evaluation question(s) (see P4, Treatment of Students; U2, Defined Users and Uses).
H. Monitor the adequacy of the information collected throughout the evaluation process (see A11, Metaevaluation).

COMMON ERRORS

A. Choosing assessment methods solely because they are available or easy to use, or because of preconceived beliefs about different assessment methods
B. Collecting information that is extraneous to the purpose of the evaluation
C. Considering the scope of information to be collected to be fixed and neglecting to respond to changes in evaluation questions or needs

Illustrative Case 1—Description

Ms. Chan, a junior high school teacher, is developing an assessment strategy to evaluate student knowledge and understanding of the scientific method. She has determined that the criteria for student mastery are "the ability to make evaluative judgments" and "the ability to provide constructive criticism." To assess these abilities, Ms. Chan has her students evaluate simulated science fair projects.

Before developing the simulated projects, Ms. Chan developed a list of errors and calculated the frequency with which they occurred in past student science fair projects. Using this list, she developed seven simulated projects. Two of these simulations were correct in all respects. The remaining five contained errors such that across the five, the frequency of the errors matched the frequency of occurrence reported in the list.

A student's ability to evaluate was determined by computing the number of errors the student correctly identified in the five simulations containing errors minus the number of errors identified in the two simulations that were error-free. The ability to provide constructive criticism was determined by the way the students identified errors and by the accuracy and feasibility of their suggestions for correcting those errors. Provision was made in the scoring key Ms. Chan developed for scoring unexpected, but justifiable, responses.

Before beginning the evaluation task, the teacher provided the students with the guidelines used by judges in previous science fairs and an outline of the way the students' responses would be scored. She discussed both of these with the students, checked that they understood both, and pointed out that criticism, when given, was to be positive and accompanied by suggestions for correcting the error(s) identified. The students then completed their evaluations and wrote an evaluation report for each project. Ms. Chan compared these reports against the key that she had developed to determine the students' abilities to evaluate and provide constructive comments and suggestions to them.

Illustrative Case 1—Analysis

Ms. Chan maintained the focus of her evaluation on the initial purposes. She developed her instruments and scoring guide so that they were relevant, reflected what occurred in practice, and avoided extraneous information. She worked to ensure that the students understood and remained on task, thereby avoiding irrelevant behaviors and allowing for valid interpretation of their scores (see A1, Validity Orientation).

Illustrative Case 2—Description

Dr. Rodgers, an instructor in a course in clinical decision making, is developing the final student assessment instrument for a program leading to a degree and certification as a licensed practitioner. He uses a selection of scenarios reproduced in the materials provided by the credentialing agency and used for licensing examinations. Because of the number of students in the class and the shortness of time, Dr. Rodgers chooses one of the easier scenarios for his final exam.

In this scenario, students are required to "take the history" of a "patient" who appears to be suffering from lower back pain. The students in this class tend to be competitive, and Dr. Rodgers has had prior experience with some students contesting their final grades based on what they claimed were inconsistencies in marking. To address this issue and enhance his reliability, he asks a colleague to score the students' responses independently. Dr. Rodgers and his colleague discuss and resolve any discrepancies before the scores are used for grading purposes.

Illustrative Case 2—Analysis

Although Dr. Rodgers addressed the issue of inconsistency in scoring, he failed to adequately assess the breadth of knowledge and skill of the students by limiting his assessment to one easy scenario. Consequently, high grades assigned to the students cannot be validly interpreted as indications that they attained the comprehensive knowledge and skills covered in the course and required by the credentialing agency (see A1, Validity Orientation; U2, Defined Users and Uses).

Dr. Rodgers needs to increase the number of test scenarios and ensure that they are representative of the knowledge and skills to be acquired by the students. He also needs to consider how to accommodate the additional scenarios to ensure that his administration and scoring procedures are practical (see F1, Practical Orientation) and yield information that is reliable (see A6, Reliable Information) and valid (see A1, Validity Orientation).

Supporting Documentation

Airasian, P. W. (1997). *Classroom assessment* (3rd ed.). New York: McGraw-Hill.

Joint Advisory Committee. (1993). *Principles for fair student assessment practices for education in Canada*. Edmonton, Alberta, Canada: University of Alberta, Centre for Research in Applied Measurement and Evaluation.

Marzano, R. J., Pickering, D., & McTighe, J. (1993). *Assessing student outcomes.* Alexandria, VA: Association for Supervision and Curriculum Development.
Reineke, R. A. (1991). Stakeholder involvement in evaluation: Suggestions for practice. *Evaluation Practice, 12,* 39-44.
Wiggins, G. P. (1993). *Assessing student performance.* San Francisco: Jossey-Bass.

U4 Evaluator Qualifications

STANDARD Teachers and others who evaluate students should have the necessary knowledge and skills, so that evaluations are carried out competently and the results can be used with confidence.

Overview

Explanation. Proper evaluations of students begin with well-qualified persons who are responsible for designing and conducting evaluations. These qualifications include the ability to

- Create or select appropriate assessments
- Collect data and information accurately
- Interpret data and information correctly
- Make and communicate sound decisions that further the educational progress of the students who are being evaluated

Because teachers are responsible for collecting most of the information about student progress, interpreting and using the information collected, and communicating the results to students and other stakeholders, they must be competent in this role.

Rationale. The acceptance and use of an evaluation depends heavily on the student's perceptions of the evaluator's expertise, professionalism, sensitivity, trustworthiness, and efficient and effective performance. If evaluators are viewed as not credible and knowledgeable about student instruction, learning, and evaluation, students may become uncooperative and passively ignore evaluation findings. Credible evaluators, on the other hand, strengthen the process and contribute to its constructive use.

Caveats. Teachers with little or no preparation for assessing and evaluating students are likely to conduct evaluations that are flawed. Given the closed nature of most classrooms and the lack of feedback on their evaluation efforts, such teachers may be comfortable with and confident about whatever evaluation skills they have. To address this issue, teachers should regularly review their evaluation practices against the recommendations made in these standards, in current textbooks, and on the Internet. They should seek assistance and mentoring from well-qualified evaluators in improving their assessment and evaluation skills.

GUIDELINES

A. Ensure that teachers and others evaluators understand effective teaching techniques and principles of learning psychology.

B. Acquire, through pre-service and in-service education, the knowledge and skills necessary to conduct meaningful student evaluations:
   - Assessment methods should be developed or chosen so that inferences drawn about the knowledge, skills, attitudes, and behaviors possessed by each student are valid and not open to misinterpretation.
   - Students should have sufficient opportunities to demonstrate their knowledge, skills, attitudes, and behavior.
   - Procedures for judging or scoring student performance should be appropriate for the assessment method used and be consistently applied and monitored.
   - Procedures for summarizing and interpreting results should yield accurate and informative representations of a student's performance in relation to the instructional goals and objectives being assessed. They should take into account the backgrounds (e.g., learning disability, English as a Second Language) and learning experiences of the students.
   - Limitations of evaluation procedures should be identified when interpreting evaluation results.
   - Evaluation reports should be clear, accurate, and of practical value to the audiences for whom they are intended.
   - Evaluation results should be used to make decisions about individual students, plan instruction, and develop curriculum.
   - Evaluators should avoid unethical, illegal, and otherwise inappropriate evaluation methods, procedures, and uses of evaluation results and findings.

C. Have other knowledgeable persons review and comment on evaluation plans and procedures before their implementation.

D. Periodically assess evaluations conducted by each evaluator.
E. Provide instructional support services to assist evaluators in being knowledgeable about their evaluations.

COMMON ERRORS

A. Failing to recognize lack of knowledge and skills needed to conduct evaluations that are fair and equitable for all students
B. Neglecting to obtain and maintain competence in all aspects of evaluation practice
C. Defending and continuing weak student evaluation practices
D. Failing to implement all scheduled evaluation activities as planned

Illustrative Case 1—Description

Mr. Brown, a high school English teacher, received a memo from the school principal saying that the school had been selected to participate in a statewide assessment of literacy, and that his grade 11 English class had been randomly chosen to participate. The testing was to take place on two days in May and instructions would follow.

Mr. Brown was not pleased about losing two instructional periods, unless it was for a good reason. He decided to inquire further about the assessment. The vice-principal was the school's liaison with the state testing agency. Mr. Brown met with him and asked the following questions:

- Why is this assessment being conducted? (He wanted to be able to tell his class why they should participate fully.)
- Who is being assessed? (He wanted some idea of the students who should participate and what, if any, guidelines or criteria were used for excluding students.)
- What is to be assessed? (He wanted to see a blueprint, so that he could fairly prepare his students.)
- What will be done with the results? (He thought both he and his students should have some useful feedback in exchange for their time.)
- Will there be any other "costs" involved? (He was concerned that the reports, whatever they might show, might have negative consequences, either for the students or for himself.)

The vice-principal's answers to the questions satisfied Mr. Brown at least to the extent that he more fully understood the purposes of the state assessment and how the data would be reported. The state was interested in the degree to which its new curriculum was achieving some more integrative outcomes, such as literacy. The results would be summarized across the state, not at the school level, and be used to inform curriculum review teams. Finally, Mr. Brown would receive a confidential report from the state testing agency describing how his class had performed relative to the rest of the state. Satisfied, he carefully read the instructions before the testing day and persuaded his students that their time and effort were worthwhile.

Illustrative Case 1—Analysis

Mr. Brown was not content to be simply a distributor of test booklets and a monitor of a testing environment. Having completed a measurement and evaluation course and having served as a marker in a previous state assessment, he knew what questions to ask. In the measurement and evaluation course, he had learned the mnemonic WWWWH (*Why* is the assessment being done? *Who* is being assessed? *What* is being assessed? *When* is the assessment to be conducted? *How* might the assessment be done?) Consequently, he took steps to find out the purposes and uses of the state assessment and gain a more complete understanding of the situation. With this understanding, Mr. Brown was able to support the aims of the assessment and encourage his students to do their best. When the class report came back to him, he was able to assess the results and interpret them, keeping in mind the purposes of the assessment and the characteristics of his class and what they had been taught.

Illustrative Case 2—Description

Ms. Sandoval, an elementary school principal, read a copy of *The Student Evaluation Standards* and became concerned that some of the teachers in her school were not fully qualified to evaluate students. She presented her concerns to the school-based teacher advisory board, which agreed to respond to the principal's concerns.

After a cursory review of the *Standards*, the advisory board teachers decided to use two standards each and try to apply them to their own evaluations in language arts. Based on their findings, they recommended that the standards be used in the school. They also believed that involving parents/guardians would be helpful. In response to that recommendation, the principal appointed a task force of teachers and parents/guardians to develop a three-year plan to increase the evaluation qualifications of teachers and help students and their parents/guardians become more competent users of student evaluation information. The task force was also asked to identify other print and Internet sources, and resource persons for learning about student evaluations.

Illustrative Case 2—Analysis

Ms. Sandoval correctly recognized that her teachers were inadequately prepared to evaluate student performance and took positive steps to correct the situation. By applying two standards each rather than the full set of standards, the teacher advisory board avoided disappointment and feelings of being overwhelmed that could easily result from trying to consider all of the standards simultaneously in the time they had to formulate their recommendations. The teachers concluded that their goal of improving student evaluations, particularly the use of evaluation information, also required involving parents/guardians. The three-year plan recognized the teachers' workloads and provided a reasonable time frame to implement the new standards without making the teachers feel overwhelmed.

Supporting Documentation

Airasian, P. W. (1991). *Classroom assessment*. New York: McGraw-Hill.

American Federation of Teachers, National Council on Measurement in Education, & National Education Association. (1990). *Standards for teacher competence in educational assessment of students*. Washington, DC: National Council on Measurement in Education.

Gullickson, A. R. (1985). Student evaluation techniques and their relationship to grade and curriculum. *Journal of Educational Research, 79*(2), 96-100.

Joint Advisory Committee. (1993). *Principles for fair student assessment practices for education in Canada*. Edmonton, Alberta, Canada: University of Alberta, Centre for Research in Applied Measurement and Evaluation.

Linn, R. L., & Gronlund, N. E. (2000). *Measurement and assessment in teaching* (8th edition). Upper Saddle River, NJ: Prentice Hall.

Stiggins, R. J. (1997). *Student-centered classroom assessment*. Upper Saddle River, NJ: Prentice Hall.

U5 Explicit Values

STANDARD In planning and conducting student evaluations, teachers and others who evaluate students should identify and justify the values used to judge student performance, so that the bases for the evaluations are clear and defensible.

Overview

Explanation. Student evaluations involve values when a state, school district, school, or individual teacher outlines the goals and objectives or learning outcomes that students are expected to acquire. Value is the root term in evaluation, and valuing is an indispensable part of student evaluation. Both the instructional program and the evaluations of students need to be clearly referenced to expected outcomes. For example, when the ability to write is an expected learning outcome, teachers should emphasize writing in their classrooms and in their student evaluations. Likewise, when teamwork or positive attitudes toward learning are valued as important outcomes, teachers should emphasize the development of teamwork and positive attitudes in both their instruction and evaluations.

Student evaluations also involve values when information and results are gathered and interpreted. Such information, whether written or numerical (see A9, Analysis of Information), will be of little interest or use if it is not interpreted against some pertinent and defensible idea of what is good and what is poor. The frame of reference used should be in accord with the type of decision to be made. Typical frames of reference used for interpretation are

- Performance in relation to pre-specified standards and rubrics (criterion-referenced interpretation)
- Performance in relation to peers (norm-referenced interpretation)

- Performance in relation to aptitude or expected growth
- Performance in terms of the amount of improvement or amount learned

If, for example, decisions are to be made about whether or not a student is ready to move on to the next unit in an instructional sequence, interpretations based on pre-specified standards would be most relevant and useful.

Before conducting a student assessment, evaluators should identify and communicate to students and other stakeholders the values used to guide the planning of a student evaluation, interpretation of the findings, and identification of appropriate follow-up activities.

Rationale. Schools are values-based institutions. They are one of society's most important instruments for sustaining and advancing culture. Society has assigned to those who work in schools the role of helping parents/guardians and the broader society educate all children and facilitate each child's intellectual, aesthetic, physical, personal, social, and vocational growth and development. Inevitably, school evaluators apply values during the assessment of each student's development and growth. They should make explicit these values and discuss them with stakeholders to ensure the acceptance of the evaluation and enhance its usefulness.

Caveats. Judging student performance and progress is complex and potentially controversial. Even when the school's mission and goals are explicit and the teacher, working from these, makes the value bases for assigned grades or other judgments explicit, there will be disagreements. Teachers and other school personnel are advised to involve students (when appropriate), parents/guardians, and other stakeholders as much as possible when developing a school's mission and goals. Together, stakeholders should clarify the values used in determining the knowledge, skills, attitudes, and behaviors that students need and in judging their performance. When this approach does not resolve a controversy, the school's staff renders the best professional judgments they can while making clear that the value bases for their judgments are consistent with the school's mission and goals.

GUIDELINES

A. Ensure that the school has a current mission statement. School administrators and teachers should develop the mission statement cooperatively with parents/guardians, students (when appropriate), and other interested members of the school community.

B. Set annual educational targets for the school that are congruent with the mission statement. All legitimate stakeholders in the school community should develop these targets cooperatively.

C. Clarify values of all of the persons who have a role in designing, implementing, and shaping the student evaluation, including those who make decisions about students.
D. Describe the procedures by which criteria will be applied to arrive at evaluative judgments before the evaluation is conducted.
E. Discuss how identified values, the evaluation procedures, and criteria for making judgments reflect sensitivity to students' gender, abilities, cultural and religious orientations, and learning disabilities.
F. Describe and justify the frame of reference for interpretation of evaluative data. Typical frames of reference are performance in relation to preset standards or rubrics, performance in relation to peers, performance in relation to aptitude, and performance in relation to amount of improvement or amount learned.

COMMON ERRORS

A. Failing to recognize alternative sources of values
B. Imposing a set of inappropriate values
C. Using evaluation criteria or procedures that are inconsistent with the prescribed values of the state, school district, and/or school

Illustrative Case 1—Description

Students at South Bay Senior High were notified during the summer that the Board of Education had approved the implementation of mathematics proficiency examinations developed and field-tested during the previous school year by an independent testing agency under contract to the Board. The tests consist of four-option multiple-choice items that assess the basic material associated with each curriculum strand for the district's mathematics program. The multiple-choice format was selected to provide quick scoring to meet the need for timely feedback to students. All students are required to pass the test to graduate. While enrolled in South Bay High, students may attempt the test as often as necessary to demonstrate proficiency. The test will be given first in October, with two additional administrations in February and May of each school year. Current juniors and seniors are exempt from the graduation requirement.

The Board of Education had been considering requiring a mathematics proficiency examination for graduation for several years. Only recently, with the addition of new board members, has there been enough political support to implement the requirement. Parents/guardians who attended board meetings supported the concept. However, only a small number of parents/guardians had attended any given board meeting. The issue of the proficiency examinations appeared on the agenda only five times in the past three years.

When parents/guardians discovered that the new graduation requirements included passing a mathematics proficiency exam, the board and district offices were besieged with angry calls. Parents/guardians felt that they had been excluded from the decision-making process. They were unaware the examination was under consideration, had not seen sample tests, and did not understand the criteria for a successful performance on the examination. Even some of the parents/guardians who supported the examination in concept were disturbed that they had not been informed of the standards for performance that their children would be expected to meet in order to graduate. During the next board meeting, more than 500 parents/guardians and their children picketed outside the building. Many were angry that the board had adopted a proficiency evaluation procedure without their knowledge or input.

Teachers also expressed displeasure with the board's decision. They had not been involved in the discussions resulting in the decision leading to the test and wondered why a proficiency examination was necessary. Although some teachers had field-tested the items, they said that they were unclear about the purpose or uses to be made of the scores. The teachers felt this was a "top-down" decision by the board, and that they should have been involved from the beginning.

Illustrative Case 1—Analysis

The Board of Education made several mistakes in its implementation of this high-stakes evaluation. Before awarding the contract for test development, the board should have provided the school community with descriptions of the values that guided their decision to use a proficiency examination. They should have explained how these values supported their selection of the multiple-choice format and why this format was superior to other formats. A table of specifications and advanced copies of sample mathematics items representative of the items to be included in the test should have been provided, so that all affected parties understood the types of skills and abilities to be evaluated. In addition, the board failed to distribute specific standards of performance that had to be met for high school graduation or to provide an adequate opportunity for students, parents/guardians, and teachers to provide feedback.

Illustrative Case 2—Description

Concerned about the low performance of its students on the state-administered assessment, the school community at Rojas Middle School, a suburban middle school, adopted the value that "All students can learn and achieve high standards." Over a period of four years, the school community worked together to develop and implement a mission statement and set annual school targets that reflected a set of values centered on students and encompassed inclusiveness, quality, and positive outcomes in terms of student development and growth. With the help of an outside facilitator, they worked through the many challenges and difficulties embedded in implementing their vision. They documented and evaluated both the process they followed and the progress they made. Although not everyone in the school community was in total agreement, a consensus was achieved about the values that underlie everything that happens in the school. Information about school policies and procedures was disseminated regularly and openly.

Rojas School is organized into multi-grade teams of four teachers per team. The curriculum is standards-based, and the faculty is in the process of developing rubrics, checklists, and other criteria for judging student performance. Students are partners in that they are responsible for their own learning and achievement. Each teacher understands how student self-assessment, team collaboration, and multiple assessment methods provide a strong database for making decisions about students. All teachers understand their ultimate responsibility for judgment within the student-centered learning environment. Professional development opportunities have addressed student assessment and evaluation, and a lead teacher and teacher-coaching program assist teachers less familiar with the student-centered approach.

Although bias and error are a part of everyday life and learning, teachers and other evaluators are confident that enough checks and balances have been built into the process through the multiple assessment approach to ensure comprehensive and consistent indications of student performance. Students report greater understanding and control over their learning, daily assessments, end-of-unit and term assessments, and decisions that affect their whole learning experience. Their parents/guardians concur.

Illustrative Case 2—Analysis

The school community at Rojas Middle School took the time to articulate and demonstrate a student-centered values orientation. The values are clear to all and provide a means for clarifying misunderstandings. They are the foundation for the curriculum and instructional approach. Policies and procedures are in place to clarify how students are assessed and evaluated, who is responsible, and by what criteria judgments are made. The values underpinning the policies and procedures serve both the needs of the school community as a whole and the individual students.

Supporting Documentation

Linn, R. L., Baker, E. L., & Dunbar, S. B. (1991). Complex, performance-based assessment: Expectations and validation criteria. *Educational Researcher, 20*(8), 15-21.

Linn, R. L., & Gronlund, N. E. (2000). *Measurement and assessment in teaching* (8th edition). Upper Saddle River, NJ: Prentice Hall.

Rorty, A. O. (Ed.). (1998). *Philosophers on education: Historical perspectives.* New York: Routledge.

Stiggins, R. J. (1997). *Student-centered classroom assessment* (2nd edition). Upper Saddle River, NJ: Prentice Hall.

U.S. Department of Education, Office for Civil Rights. (2000). *The use of tests as part of high-stakes decision-making for students: A resource guide for educators and policy-makers*. Washington, DC: Author. Retrieved May 17, 2002, from http://www.ed.gov/offices/OCR/testing/.

U6 Effective Reporting

STANDARD Student evaluation reports should be clear, timely, accurate, and relevant, so that they are useful to students, their parents/guardians, and other legitimate users.

Overview

Explanation. Students and other stakeholders need information about students' progress and level of attainment in school. Whether the reported evaluation information is influential and the extent to which it is used depends on four factors: clarity, timeliness, accuracy, and relevance.

Clarity means that the report is free from ambiguity and is written in a way that can be understood by the student, parents, or others who will receive it. For example, reports should use language and terms familiar to the intended audiences and be free of jargon and irrelevant information.

Timeliness means that the student or other user receives the report at the time it is needed, so that the information can be used in intended ways. For example, the student should be provided evaluation information to facilitate knowledge and/or skill development before being held accountable on a final exam.

Accuracy means the report is free from errors. To achieve accuracy, reports must be based on sound data and should be free of errors caused by bias, insufficient supporting information, or vague wording that could lead to misinterpretation (see A1, Validity Orientation) and cause possible harm to the student (see P4, Treatment of Students).

Relevance means that the evaluative information meets the needs of the users. For example, a test grade alone may address accountability needs, but more information must be provided to serve student learning (e.g., interpretations of probable student misunderstandings). To encourage follow-up, reports should identify both strengths and weaknesses, so that strengths can be built upon and weaknesses addressed (see P6, Balanced Evaluation).

The reporting system for a school or jurisdiction should be guided by a written policy. Elements to consider include such aspects as audiences, reporting medium, format, content, level of detail, frequency, timing, and confidentiality. The community of stakeholders should develop the reporting policy. Cooperative interaction not only leads to better reporting, but also increases the likelihood that the reports will be understood and used by those for whom they are intended.

Rationale. When reports are clear, timely, accurate, and relevant, they will not be ends in themselves, but instruments leading to student progress and improvement. None of the factors can be reduced or missing and still result in a fully useful report. For example, good evaluation information received too late cannot serve student learning. Similarly, a timely report that is deficient in other ways (i.e., not accurate, not understandable, or not relevant) will have reduced value. Depending upon the type and extent of its deficiencies, the report can harm those it is intended to serve. For example, reports overemphasizing faults and weaknesses in a student or those offering unqualified praise reduce the validity and utility of the evaluation.

Caveats. Often, the need for immediate feedback to continuously direct and motivate student learning precludes preparation of extended formal reports for students. These informal assessments occur quickly and directly between the teacher and student and are most often verbal. Even under these informal conditions, the teacher should carefully consider what he or she says, and say it in ways that are most likely to encourage appropriate decisions and actions on the part of the student.

GUIDELINES

A. Prepare a written policy to guide the reporting system for a school or jurisdiction.

B. Design student reports to facilitate student learning:
- Include a description of the goals and objectives of instruction to which the evaluation is referenced.
- Provide clear, concrete, and accurate feedback, including specific strengths and weaknesses with suggestions for improvement in problem areas (see U7, Follow-Up).
- Avoid the use of unfamiliar terms and jargon. Explain what letter grades and other symbols mean and how they should be interpreted and used.
- Allow enough time to prepare and check the completeness and accuracy of formal reports before they are shared with users.

- Design reports to enhance clarity, readability, and understandability.
- Provide for conferences between teachers and parents. Whenever it is appropriate, students should participate in these conferences.
- Describe to students and their parents/guardians the process they may use to appeal a report.

C. Indicate to users how the report may be useful to them, how the evaluation was conducted, how the data support the interpretations and recommendations (see A5, Defensible Information), and how the findings may be used to further the educational development of the students (see U7, Follow-Up).

D. Determine if the report should be retained in the student's file for future use (e.g., to assist in measuring growth over time) and whether the student's report in whole or in part should contribute to other decision situations (e.g., at the school or district level).

E. Maintain confidentiality in reporting (see P3, Access to Evaluation Information).

F. Use a variety of approaches to reporting (e.g., report cards with a portfolio and a student-led conference).

G. Produce timely reports, so that information provided will be of maximum use.

H. Explain to users how reports may be useful to them, why and how the evaluation was conducted, and how the data support the interpretations and recommendations.

I. Obtain feedback from users on the usefulness, clarity, timeliness, and accuracy of reports they have received (see A11, Metaevaluation).

COMMON ERRORS

A. Failing to sufficiently involve the recipients of reports, particularly students and their parents/guardians, in the evaluation process to make the reports meaningful and relevant

B. Overemphasizing either strengths or weaknesses through use of excessive detail or misleading information

C. Distorting the report by seeking to provide equal amounts of positive and negative feedback

D. Failing to share reports with relevant audiences, so they could all benefit from the information (see P1, Service to Students).

Illustrative Case 1—Description

In addition to sending a report card home, Ms. Diddens, a middle school mathematics teacher, provides reports to parents/guardians through parent-teacher conferences. Because she has several sections of mathematics, she relies on numerical scores from tests and homework for evaluating students in her classes. These scores are stored on her computer for easy retrieval.

During each parent-teacher conference, Ms. Diddens sits in front of the computer with the student's parents/guardians nearby, so that she can show them their child's test and homework scores and the sum of these scores for the grading period. She runs her finger along the row of scores for the student, so that parents/guardians can see the child's data. Ms. Diddens then shifts the screen to a graph of the distribution of the total scores for all her mathematics students and shows the parents/guardians the place on the graph where their child falls. She then answers any questions from the parents/guardians. Parents/guardians who cannot attend the conferences receive a copy of their children's mathematics scores. However, these parents/guardians are left to interpret the results themselves.

Several parents/guardians, some of whom attended the parent-teacher conference and others who did not, called Ms. Diddens to say that they did not understand her reports or her evaluation system, and that they had heard that other parents/guardians had seen their children's marks.

Illustrative Case 1—Analysis

Whereas parents who attended conferences received marginally adequate information, parents who did not attend received inadequate information. Ms. Diddens needs to prepare better reports that more clearly connect student scores to goals and objectives of instruction and indicate what students have accomplished and what they need to work on in order to be successful. She also needs to be more proactive in anticipating parent/guardian needs and in suggesting appropriate follow-up actions for student improvement.

The way in which the scores were presented to the parents/guardians of each student violated the confidentiality of other students. Parents/guardians were able to read on the computer screen not only the scores of their own child, but also those of other students. Ms. Diddens needs to respect confidentiality by presenting the scores for each child in such a way that the marks of other students are not visible.

Illustrative Case 2—Description

The students in a cooking class at a Centerville Junior High School were preparing to complete their first laboratory experience. During the lab, which involved mixing and baking chocolate chip cookies, the students worked in groups. The intent was to have the students learn how to work cooperatively, as well as how to make cookies. During the lab, the teacher moved about the room, observing what the students were doing and recording her observations on a checklist she developed. Provision was made for recording information for each student and for each group of students.

After the laboratory experience ended, the teacher met with each learning group to evaluate its performance and assign grades. Each student received an individual grade, a group grade, and a full explanation of these grades. The teacher then met with each student separately to further discuss the grades the student received and to provide an opportunity for the student to seek clarification and ask questions. During the following class, the students were provided with general feedback regarding their abilities to work cooperatively and suggestions for improving their performance during the next cooperative laboratory experience.

Illustrative Case 2—Analysis

The teacher effectively reported the results of the student evaluations, because she directed the results to the appropriate persons in a timely way. In addition, she clarified grades, provided students with information relevant to improved performance on similar activities, and provided an opportunity for the students to discuss their own performances individually.

Supporting Documentation

Airasian, P. W. (1997). *Classroom assessment* (3rd edition). New York: McGraw-Hill.

Cangelosi, J. S. (2000). *Assessment strategies for monitoring student learning.* New York: Addison Wesley Longman.

Joint Advisory Committee. (1993). *Principles for fair student assessment practices for education in Canada.* Edmonton, Alberta, Canada: University of Alberta, Centre for Research in Applied Measurement and Evaluation.

Joint Committee on Testing Practices. (1998). *Code for fair testing practices for education.* Washington, DC: American Psychological Association.

Ministry of Education. (1994). *Guidelines for student reporting for the Kindergarten to Grade 12 Education Plan*. Victoria, BC, Canada: Author.

O'Connor, K. (1999). *The mindful school: How to grade for learning*. Arlington Heights, IL: Skylight.

Stiggins, R. J. (1997). *Student-centered classroom assessment* (2nd edition). Upper Saddle River, NJ: Prentice Hall.

U7 Follow-Up

STANDARD Student evaluations should include procedures for follow-up, so that students, parents/guardians, and other legitimate users can understand the information and take appropriate follow-up actions.

Overview

Explanation. Student evaluations should include procedures to help students and other stakeholders take appropriate actions based on the assessment. Teachers should work with students and, where appropriate, their parents/guardians and other stakeholders (e.g., school counselors) to design appropriate plans to assist students in overcoming weaknesses while reinforcing strengths. For example, they might suggest suitable reading materials for a beginning student reader, a study guide for a high school student, or the use of a tutor for a junior high student. In follow-up, the evaluator verifies that the stakeholders have received the evaluation information, understand it, can see potential for improvement, and recognize that follow-up actions have been identified.

Rationale. Evaluators should recognize that no matter how sound the evaluation, its value lies in the use of its findings. Follow-up activities should be included as a regular part of the evaluation process. Merely presenting results in the form of a report card or at a parent-teacher conference diminishes the potential positive impact a well-designed and conducted evaluation can have. Well-planned, relevant follow-up will help avoid misinterpretation of evaluation findings and encourage their use to improve student learning and performance.

Caveats. The users of evaluation information should not assume that improvements will happen automatically. Teachers should be prepared to assist students and other stakeholders in assessing and using evaluation results. Some follow-up processes require time (e.g., developing literacy skills), whereas others may require only brief attention (e.g., reviewing course concepts).

GUIDELINES

A. Design, in consultation with students and their parents/guardians, relevant follow-up activities (e.g., homework, tutor, study buddy) that address areas for weakness while maintaining areas of strength.

B. Monitor the effects of follow-up to ensure improvement in student performance and to avoid possible negative side effects (e.g., concentrating on one subject to the detriment of other subjects).

COMMON ERRORS

A. Assuming that students, parents, and other users will understand and use evaluation information

B. Prescribing follow-up activities that are unrealistic for the student and his or her parents/guardians

Illustrative Case 1—Description

Mrs. Johnson teaches algebra at Springfield High School. Yesterday's lesson on quadratic equations seemed to go as planned. However, as she graded the homework, she found many students making similar errors. The next day, Mrs. Johnson handed back the homework with errors corrected and then reinforced the previous day's lesson. After the supplemental instruction, she assigned more problems during the remaining class time and monitored student progress before assigning more homework.

When she collected the second homework assignment, Mrs. Johnson found that her follow-up to the initial homework evaluation had proved beneficial. All but two of the students who had made errors on previous assignments were able to complete the new homework error free. Most students were able to apply their understanding of the concept of quadratic equations in subsequent lessons. For the two students who continued to have difficulty, Mrs. Johnson arranged a tutorial session with another student who had a strong understanding of both quadratic equations and the particular techniques being taught.

Illustrative Case 1—Analysis

Mrs. Johnson evaluated homework in a timely fashion. When she found similar errors in many students' work, she wisely decided to make her students aware of the nature of the errors, provide reinforcement, monitor their progress in class, and assign more homework. The short-term follow-up allowed the students to acquire the concepts needed for subsequent applications. For the two students who continued to have difficulties, her additional follow-up helped ensure that they learned the concept. Furthermore, it demonstrated her commitment to helping all students learn.

Illustrative Case 2—Description

At the beginning of the school year, Ms. Mancini, a second-grade teacher, organized parent volunteers who read with the students. Early in the term, she noticed that Allison, one of her students, was experiencing difficulty in reading fluently. Rather than wait until the first reporting period, she called Allison's parents and requested a conference. There she explained their daughter's lack of progress. Ms. Mancini asked the parents what they were doing at home with regard to reading. They said that they had Allison read aloud to one of them every night. Through additional discussion, Ms. Mancini discovered that when Allison came to a word she did not know, her parents had her sound it out. Ms. Mancini then suggested that they try an approach in which fluency of reading is stressed. She discussed research that had shown how with this approach both reading rate and comprehension increased.

Allison's parents agreed to try the new reading strategy. Ms. Mancini described the approach, gave them a videocassette that illustrated the procedure, and arranged for the volunteer parent readers at the school to use the new approach. She also gave the parents the level of reader most suitable for Allison, so that they could borrow appropriate books from the public library to work with her at home.

Illustrative Case 2—Analysis

Ms. Mancini, working with her parent volunteers, was able to quickly diagnose Allison's reading difficulty. Rather than wait until the first reporting period, she properly arranged a parent-teacher conference. During this conference, she provided information in an understandable way and suggested a practical, low-cost, follow-up action that would require little change in their reading activities at home. This early follow-up with the parents likely reinforced parental involvement in learning and promptly addressed the student's reading problem.

Supporting Documentation

Airasian, P. W. (1997). *Classroom assessment* (3rd edition). New York: McGraw-Hill.

Cangelosi, J. S. (2000). *Assessment strategies for monitoring student learning*. New York: Longman.

Stiggins, R. J. (1997). *Student-centered classroom assessment* (2nd edition). Upper Saddle River, NJ: Prentice Hall.

FEASIBILITY STANDARDS

Summary of the Standards

F Feasibility Standards The feasibility standards help ensure that student evaluations can be implemented as planned. Feasible evaluations are practical, diplomatic, and adequately supported. These standards are as follows:

F1 Practical Orientation Student evaluation procedures should be practical, so that they produce the needed information in efficient, nondisruptive ways.

F2 Political Viability Student evaluations should be planned and conducted with the anticipation of questions from students, their parents/guardians, and other legitimate users, so that their questions can be answered effectively and their cooperation obtained.

F3 Evaluation Support Adequate time and resources should be provided for student evaluations, so that evaluations can be effectively planned and implemented, their results fully communicated, and appropriate follow-up activities identified.

F1 Practical Orientation

STANDARD Student evaluation procedures should be practical, so that they produce the needed information in efficient, nondisruptive ways.

Overview

Explanation. Practical procedures provide data and information that can be validly interpreted without disrupting the instructional sequence or impeding learning. These procedures should be efficient and ethical. Student evaluation procedures comprise the series of actions taken to address and promote student achievement, behavior, and other factors important to student learning and growth. These procedures include the following:

- Identifying the purpose of the evaluation
- Identifying the likely use of the data and information to be collected
- Developing or selecting an assessment strategy relevant to the purpose and use of the evaluation
- Collecting the assessment information
- Scoring the students' responses
- Interpreting the scores obtained
- Aggregating the individual assessment results to form summary comments and grades
- Reporting information to students and other stakeholders
- Designing and implementing follow-up actions.

Rationale. Students must be provided with full opportunities to demonstrate the knowledge and skills they have acquired, so that sound judgments can be made about their performances. Steps must be taken to ensure that adequate resources and time for the evaluation are available. Impractical procedures can be inefficient and needlessly disruptive, detracting from students' performance and taking away instructional time. They can also diminish the credibility of the teacher and lower student morale. Consequently, teachers should work to ensure that their evaluation procedures are not cumbersome, overly burdensome, overly complex, needlessly obtrusive, or superficial.

Caveats. When developing evaluation procedures, consider the consequences of the decisions to be made. The outcomes of some evaluations will be more critical than the outcomes of others. For example, misinterpretation of the performance on an end-of-unit test may result in incorrectly holding a student from moving to the next instructional unit in a continuous progress situation. In such high-stakes situations, every effort should be made to ensure that the evaluation procedures will yield consistent and valid results (see A6, Reliable Information; A1, Validity Orientation). Furthermore, the procedures should be written in direct and familiar language, so that the intended evaluation process is clearly understood. Once written, the procedures can be inspected should the need arise due to an appeal of a result. Low-stakes situations, such as determining if a student has correctly completed an in-class assignment, can be less stringent.

GUIDELINES

A. Develop evaluation priorities and align student evaluation practices with those priorities to ensure that the most important evaluation matters are effectively addressed.
B. Identify potential positive and negative consequences of an evaluation before designing the evaluation procedures (see U2, Defined Users and Uses).
C. Ensure that assessment methods are clearly related to the purposes of the evaluation, are compatible with the instructional approaches used, and minimize disruption in the instructional sequence.
D. Organize and describe the evaluation process clearly and chronologically, so that students and other stakeholders can easily understand and follow the progression.
E. List materials needed for the assessment method and obtain and organize them so there will be no disruption during data collection.
F. Develop valid alternate procedures for collecting assessment information from students with learning disabilities and students whose proficiency in the language of instruction is inadequate for them to respond in the anticipated manner (see P4, Treatment of Students).
G. Develop understandable procedures for scoring, reporting, decision making, and follow-up (see A4, Documented Procedures; U7, Follow-Up).

H. Establish procedures to protect the confidentiality of students' evaluative data and results (see P3, Access to Evaluation Information).

COMMON ERRORS

A. Assuming that student evaluation procedures are relevant to the goals and objectives of instruction and aligned with the curriculum
B. Assuming that all assessment methods can be simply and easily implemented
C. Using short-cut assessment procedures to economize on resources at the expense of accuracy
D. Failing to consider situational factors that may influence student performance (e.g., student fatigue, physical conditions, and timing)
E. Disrupting ongoing instruction with "ritualistic" testing

Illustrative Case 1—Description

In the Green Mountain School District, a rural school district that practices standards-based education, the performance on state writing assessments revealed that the district's mean scores for writing were slightly below the state mean. In response, the school board allocated resources to develop and implement its own annual assessment of writing in grades 3, 6, 9, and 12 in an attempt to improve the writing performance of the students.

The board assigned the task to the district curriculum director with instructions to involve teachers and members of the community in the evaluation process. The curriculum director then formed a writing team comprised of selected elementary school teachers who taught grades 3 or 6 and secondary language arts teachers who taught grades 9 or 12. She involved the community by forming a marking team consisting of parents/guardians, education students from the local college, and community members interested in education.

Working with the curriculum director, the writing team developed writing tasks and scoring rubrics aligned with the district's emphasis on writing and reflecting the areas of weakness and strengths identified from results of the state assessment. They then prepared a guide explaining the purpose of the new assessment and how to administer and score the writing tasks. These materials were distributed to all the elementary teachers teaching grades 3 and 6 and secondary language arts teachers teaching grades 9 and 12. Teachers were encouraged to contact a member of the writing team should they have questions. No questions or comments were forthcoming. Furthermore, a check of a sample of teachers showed that the teachers understood the purpose and nature of the district's writing assessment.

As a way of involving all teachers of students who would be assessed, the teachers were allowed to determine the time (days/class periods) of administration and the writing prompt to be used for the assessment in their classroom. Following the guidelines provided, teachers explained the assessment procedure to their students and described the scoring rubric that would be used to mark the papers. They also explained that student papers would be marked twice, once by themselves and once by someone from the marking team. They encouraged the students to do their best work, because the scores would be included in their final grade. The assessment took place over two days and was conducted in the students' regular classrooms.

The teachers scored their students' papers using the scoring rubric and discussed the results with the students before they sent the papers to the district office. The marking team then scored the papers. Tables, each accommodating four markers, were set up in the high school gymnasium, so that all the marking could be completed in a common place. The marking session began with training conducted by members of the writing team. The rubric was applied to three sample papers and the scoring of these papers was discussed. Markers were cautioned to respect student confidentiality and keep the scores secure. Each person was then assigned a group of papers to score. The writing team members monitored the scoring and answered questions as they arose.

Illustrative Case 1—Analysis

The writing assessment, as implemented, was practical, causing minimal disruption for teachers and students. The writing tasks were designed to meet the purpose of the assessment and were meaningful to the teachers in the district. Teachers at the grade levels at which the assessment was conducted understood the purpose and nature of the evaluation and were involved in realistic ways in administering the writing task and scoring the responses. The physical setting was familiar to the students. Students knew in advance how they would be assessed and how the results would be used. The community at large was involved through the marking team, thereby providing them with firsthand knowledge of the students' performances.

Illustrative Case 2—Description

Mr. Rizzo, a new fourth-grade teacher, was interested in evaluating how well his fourth-grade students understood science. He decided to develop a performance assessment. He modeled his procedure after the multiple-station approach used at the state level that he learned about in his science methods class at college.

Mr. Rizzo set up six stations, each designed to measure one of the science outcomes for grade 4. He arranged for adequate distance between adjacent stations, and placed what he believed to be sufficient amounts of the perishable materials at each station where the materials were to be used. He developed an observation checklist for assessment. To facilitate the evaluation, he split the class in half. The first group took the assessment on one day and the second group on the next day. He provided computer work related to science for the students not engaged in the performance assessment.

Two unanticipated problems arose during the performance assessment on the first day. First, several students needed additional time at one or more stations. Consequently, students who had completed their station were left with nothing to do. Second, perishable materials critical to the performance at some stations were not always replenished quickly. Again, the students were left with nothing to do. Consequently, Mr. Rizzo spent most of his time running from station to station and attending to behavior problems instead of making the observations he had planned.

Illustrative Case 2—Analysis

Performance assessment is a complex undertaking. The design Mr. Rizzo followed was developed for state assessments. Mr. Rizzo did not have the knowledge and experience to deal with such a complex assessment procedure in his classroom. He misjudged the time needed to complete the task at each station and the rate at which perishable materials would be used up. To eliminate these problems, Mr. Rizzo should have pilot-tested his stations or adopted stations that had been used in the state assessment. Furthermore, he should have had assistants (a teacher's aide or two or three students from higher grades) who could help replenish the perishable materials and monitor the students, leaving him free to make observations. Finally, testing different students on different days may have given an unintended advantage to the students assessed on the second day, because they knew what to expect and because some or all of the problems encountered on the first day were resolved on the second day.

Supporting Documentation

Airasian, P. W. (1997). *Classroom assessment* (3rd edition). New York: McGraw-Hill.

Marzano, R. J., Pickering, D., & McTighe, J. (1993). *Assessing student outcomes.* Alexandria, VA: Association for Supervision and Curriculum Development.

Perrone, V. (Ed.). (1991). *Expanding student assessment.* Alexandria, VA: Association for Supervision and Curriculum Development.
Tierney, R. J., Carter, M. A., & Desai, L. E. (1991). *Portfolio assessment in the reading-writing classroom.* Norwood, MA: Christopher-Gordon.
Wiggins, G. P. (1993). *Assessing student performance.* San Francisco: Jossey-Bass.

F2 Political Viability

STANDARD Student evaluations should be planned and conducted with the anticipation of questions from students, their parents/guardians, and other legitimate users, so that their questions can be answered effectively and their cooperation obtained.

Overview

Explanation. An evaluation has political implications to the extent that it leads to decisions about a student's attainment and that these decisions have consequences for the student's future progress (e.g., placement into programs, promotion to the next grade, high school graduation). Consequently, student evaluation policies and guidelines should allow all stakeholders to gain a common understanding of the purposes and procedures of the evaluations. Evaluators should conduct the assessments with the goal of fully informing students and their parents/guardians of identified strengths and weaknesses in learning, so that strengths can be built upon and weaknesses addressed. Classroom teachers and, where appropriate, administrators, counselors, and learning resource teachers should be willing to work with parents/guardians to take constructive follow-up actions (see U7, Follow-Up).

Rationale. If evaluation purposes and procedures are understandable, and if students and other stakeholders can ask questions and seek clarification about the evaluations, then they are more likely to support the evaluation process and trust and use the evaluation findings. Teachers and administrators need to create a climate that will encourage stakeholders to ask questions and seek clarification. If conditions are not politically viable, misunderstandings, noncooperation, and/or noncompliance are likely to occur. At best, poor political viability will result in evaluations that do not fully serve the students. At worst, the evaluations will be detrimental to students.

Caveats. Political viability often competes directly with efficiency. It can be time-consuming and costly to involve stakeholders in an evaluation, answer questions, and clarify evaluation issues they raise. The effort to achieve political viability will likely be commensurate with the consequences of the decisions to be made. Some decisions (e.g., determining if a student has completed an in-class assignment) are much less politically sensitive than others (e.g., deciding standards for graduation or selection into the school's honor society).

GUIDELINES

A. Develop written policies to guide student evaluations. Teachers, administrators, and other school personnel should develop these policies in consultation with students, parents/guardians, and other persons entitled to receive evaluation findings and reports.
B. Involve all stakeholders, to the extent possible, in the planning and development of student evaluations. Consider representation from a wide range of groups (e.g., racial, ethnic, cultural, and linguistic minority groups) and ensure gender balance.
C. Clarify in writing who has the authority to make final decisions.
D. Ensure that the evaluation is conducted in a sound and credible manner.
E. Rectify problems in the conduct of a student evaluation promptly and effectively.
F. Obtain regular feedback from students, parents/guardians, teachers, administrators, and other appropriate users, and respond to their questions and concerns promptly (see P1, Service to Students; U1, Constructive Orientation; and A12, Metaevaluation). Use the feedback to revise and improve evaluation procedures.
G. Maintain confidentiality of student information and evaluation results (see P5, Rights of Students).
H. Obtain parent/guardian permission when needed for an evaluation (see P5, Rights of Students).

COMMON ERRORS

A. Failing to provide sufficient time for students and other stakeholders to ask questions and seek clarification about an evaluation
B. Failing to treat all persons who ask questions or seek clarification equally and with respect
C. Assuming that silence from stakeholders implies approval of evaluation policies and procedures

D. Failing to acknowledge the limitations presented by the assessment methods used, problems encountered in collecting the information, judging or scoring procedures, and data interpretation

Illustrative Case 1—Description

Ms. Taylor, an elementary school principal, wanted to implement a new assessment program for reading, writing, and mathematics to supplement the district's standardized testing program. She and the school's guidance counselor attended a session on portfolio assessment offered at the state assessment conference. They then did a literature search on the use and benefits of portfolio assessment. Based on what they had learned, Ms. Taylor and the guidance counselor designed a system that was to include portfolio assessment in addition to the multiple-choice and essay tests already used to measure ongoing student progress. The new system was to document student progress for purposes of improving instruction and teacher accountability.

Ms. Taylor called a meeting of grade-level chairpersons and informed them of the proposed addition to the current evaluation plan. She sought their comments on the plan and how they might pilot the new procedures schoolwide. To ensure community support, Ms. Taylor invited parents/guardians to an informal evening meeting to introduce the concept of portfolio assessment. Because she did not want to impose on teachers to have to return to the school in the evening (or pay for the additional teacher time), Ms. Taylor did not invite school staff to this meeting. A few parents/guardians and teachers did attend the meeting. After Ms. Taylor and the guidance counselor answered questions and addressed their concerns, the parents/guardians who attended the meeting seemed to support the evaluation plan. The teachers, having been told earlier by their grade-level chairpersons that the program would be pilot-tested, did not speak.

Based on the support of her department chairs and the parents/guardians who attended the meeting, Ms. Taylor implemented the program. She sent a memo to the staff telling them to meet with their grade chairpersons to learn about the procedures for implementing the new, mandatory portfolio assessment system. The chairpersons provided teachers with a memo prepared by Ms. Taylor and the guidance counselor that outlined the portfolio assessment procedures. However, many teachers pointed out that they had had little experience or professional development in using portfolio assessments. Others were concerned that the portfolio system required substantial work, was of limited usefulness, and created potential practical problems for them. Many of the teachers were upset and unwilling to support the new evaluation system.

Illustrative Case 1—Analysis

While Ms. Taylor sought input and feedback from her staff in leadership positions and from the parents/guardians who attended the informational meeting, she did not solicit comments from the teachers who would actually implement the new program. She changed the intended emphasis from using portfolios to supplement the assessment methods already in place to one that emphasized the primary use of portfolios. She also failed to ensure that the teachers were qualified to evaluate portfolios. Consequently, the unwillingness of the teachers to cooperate and comply with her desire to implement portfolios is understandable.

Ms. Taylor could have gained the cooperation of the teachers had she involved the entire teaching staff or at least a greater number of representatives from the teaching staff in planning the new program. She could have introduced the new assessment plan at a faculty meeting and asked volunteers to form a planning team. She also could have surveyed the staff to determine the need for an in-service workshop on portfolios.

By involving teachers before announcing the mandatory plan, she could have addressed the teachers' concerns and needs proactively and incorporated their knowledge and experiences in the new plan. Such an inclusive approach would have increased the political viability of the proposed evaluation plan and led to greater cooperation and compliance.

Illustrative Case 2—Description

Ms. St. Clair, a new physics teacher in a large suburban high school, was assigned to teach advanced physics. The course content was challenging for the high school seniors, and there were many required experiments. Because the course was new for her, Ms. St. Clair asked Mr. Rosenberg, the physics teacher who had taught the course for the past five years, if she could use exams he had given to guide her in the development of her own examinations. She was concerned that there be continuity in the way the students were evaluated in this course.

Mr. Rosenberg gave Ms. St. Clair the tests and final examination he had used, the table of specifications for each test and the final, the scoring keys, and the results of item analyses he had conducted for each test and the final. He suggested that she use the scoring guides for the required laboratory experiments, because they would be the same. Together, they decided that she would use the same table of specifications for her tests and final and that her tests should include some of the items from his examinations in addition to new items that she would construct. This would allow for the continuity she desired.

During the semester, Ms. St. Clair compared the lab, test, and final exam results from her students with the results Mr. Rosenberg had obtained with his. She found that their results of the item analyses were comparable. No students in the class complained. They recognized that the labs, tests, and final examination she gave were similar to those that had been administered in previous years.

Illustrative Case 2—Analysis

Ms. St. Clair, as a new teacher, wisely decided to ensure explicitly that the assessment procedures she used were comparable to those used in previous years. At the same time, her workload was reduced by using, at least in part, materials already prepared and shown to have worked (see F1, Practical Orientation). Had she struck out on her own, drastic differences may have occurred, and her workload would have been greater.

Supporting Documentation

American Educational Research Association, American Psychological Association, & National Council on Measurement in Education. (1999). *Standards for educational and psychological testing*. Washington, DC: American Educational Research Association.

Moss, P. A., & Schutz, A. (1999). Risking frankness in educational assessment. *Phi Delta Kappan, 80*(9), 680-687.

O'Malley, J. M., & Valdez-Pierce, L. (1996). *Authentic assessment for English language learners: Practical approaches for teachers*. Reading, MA: Addison-Wesley.

U.S. Department of Education, Office for Civil Rights. (2000). *The use of tests as part of high-stakes decision-making for students: A resource guide for educators and policy-makers*. Washington, DC: Author. Retrieved May 17, 2002, from http://www.ed.gov/offices/OCR/testing/.

F3 Evaluation Support

STANDARD Adequate time and resources should be provided for student evaluations, so that evaluations can be effectively planned and implemented, their results fully communicated, and appropriate follow-up activities identified.

Overview

Explanation. Student evaluations require resources to ensure that the data and information obtained can be meaningfully used to further the educational development of students. Teachers require adequate time to develop evaluation plans, conduct assessments, analyze and interpret student data, report findings to students and their parents/guardians, and plan follow-up activities. Students need adequate time and help to prepare for and respond to the assessment. Both students and their parents/guardians may need assistance in using evaluation feedback to develop appropriate follow-up actions.

Teachers need to be trained and kept abreast of new developments in the field of student evaluation if they are to conduct sound and credible evaluations (see U4, Evaluator Qualifications). Professional development in the form of coordinated in-service education, perhaps supplemented with assessment support on the Internet, should be encouraged and supported. Other possible resources include the following:

- Item and performance task banks that teachers can use to develop assessments
- Computer-based record keeping
- Materials and assistants for performance assessments
- Secretarial support for preparation and duplication of assessments

- Assistance in analyzing the qualities of assessment instruments (e.g., item analysis)
- Assistance in interpreting external standardized test results

Rationale. All teachers are expected to conduct evaluations to assist and support student learning and development and ensure student and teacher accountability. These evaluations are not resource-free. Resource allocation is a visible demonstration of a school system's commitment to student evaluation. Adequate resources and support improve the possibility for success. Without them, an evaluation effort is prone to inappropriate compromises, shortcuts, and omissions. When limited resources hamper sound, efficient evaluation practices, evaluation results are likely to be of limited influence or to have negative consequences for students, their parents/guardians, teachers, and the school.

Caveats. School administrators and teachers must carefully allocate resources to best serve their evaluation needs. Expectations for student evaluations must be balanced against the resources supplied in order to provide evaluations that yield consistent, valid, and useful information. However, resource support alone will not guarantee a successful student evaluation program. Teachers, students, and other stakeholders must use these resources effectively, the evaluations must be integrated into instruction, and the results must be used productively.

GUIDELINES

A. Identify the purpose(s) of the evaluation and how the resulting information will be used (see U2, Defined Users and Uses).
B. Ensure that the resources and support available are sufficient to achieve the evaluation purposes.
C. Estimate the time and financial costs of needed assessment resources such as materials, secretarial support, teacher assistants, and computer and analysis support.
D. Estimate the personnel time required to conduct each type of assessment and use the estimates to decide on the frequency and feasibility of each assessment method.
E. Ensure that the resources for evaluations are used effectively and efficiently.
F. Search for new ideas that will help teachers achieve evaluations that serve the educational development of students.

COMMON ERRORS

A. Avoiding assessment methods that—although time-consuming, difficult to conduct, or costly—yield important data

B. Failing to allocate enough resources to allow for evaluations of students in a timely, accurate, and acceptable manner
C. Failing to allocate sufficient time and financial resources to provide appropriate training to teachers (see U4, Evaluator Qualifications) and users of student evaluations (see U7, Follow-Up)
D. Wasting resources on collecting irrelevant data or conducting poorly developed evaluations
E. Failing to include the costs for assistance in analyzing the quality of assessment instruments (e.g., item analysis) and interpreting external standardized test results

Illustrative Case 1—Description

Dr. Ramesh, a college professor, is currently testing a student evaluation strategy that he believes has merit for all levels of instruction. The strategy is resource intensive and requires a large pool of items that covers the entire course content, with each major segment covered by at least five items. The item pool must be divided by content category. The strategy also requires computer-based support for analysis. A person may be needed to assist in scoring and analyzing data. Finally, some class time is required each week to administer five-minute quizzes and share the results with the students.

Dr. Ramesh's strategy is as follows. The large pool of items is divided in half, with each half fully representing the course content and objectives. One half is set aside and kept secure to be used for the final exam. The other half is randomly divided into small quizzes. Each quiz has approximately the same number of items and randomly approximates the expected content coverage. Quizzes can be administered in five minutes. The quizzes are given to five students, and each student receives a different quiz each week. The procedure dictates that each set of weekly quizzes covers the full content of the course.

Each week, the professor summarizes the results of all quizzes on a topic-by-topic basis. No student is graded on quiz results. Instead, the quizzes are used as a barometer of student learning. As content is covered in class, scores for that content area are expected to improve and show class mastery of the topic. If learning did not occur as expected, the quiz results are used to identify instruction and learning problems. If scores decline on a topic after initial mastery, the instructor provides feedback to students and assigns additional homework to reinforce earlier learning.

Illustrative Case 1—Analysis

Although testing of this strategy is still at an early stage, Dr. Ramesh's approach is an example of the kinds of student evaluation practices that can be used and the potential benefits obtained when adequate resources are committed to student evaluation. For example, although the strategy requires significant planning before instruction begins and continued work during the course, it benefits students by providing a low-stakes method to assess their understanding and progress in the course and by identifying topics that need reinforcement. The teacher gains by learning about student progress and the effectiveness of his instruction in a timely and time-efficient manner.

Illustrative Case 2—Description

Mr. Hernandez, an eighth-grade social studies teacher, developed a strategy for conducting regular chapter and unit tests of course content. Concerned about the amount of time taken from instruction to give these tests, he determined that time, as a resource, should be the same for all students being tested. As a result, he established the rule that all students would have the same amount of time to complete tests. All students started each test at the same time, and when the first student finished, all students were required to stop. This strategy reduced the amount of time required for testing and provided more time for instruction.

Illustrative Case 2—Analysis

Time is a vital resource for both instruction and evaluation. Mr. Hernandez's strategy gives equal time to all students for completion of the test and limits the time required for testing. However, there are serious concerns with his approach. Instructional time may have been increased and time costs for evaluation decreased, but other important considerations and desired outcomes from student testing were ignored or placed at risk.

This method does not provide all students with adequate time to perform to their best ability on the exams (see P4, Treatment of Students). Because students read, think, and work at different speeds, this strategy rewards those who work quickly, but not necessarily thoughtfully. It penalizes those who work more slowly, but perhaps with more diligence. It further penalizes any special needs students whose disability restricts the speed at which they can work. This confuses the interpretation of the scores and is likely to compromise their validity (see A1, Validity Orientation). The result is likely to be student disenchantment with social studies, a focus on rote memory and knowledge, and substantial loss of rapport within the classroom (e.g., student animosity toward the student who completes the test first). Mr. Hernandez failed to consider all the outcomes of his evaluation and the linkages between these outcomes and resources before he made his decision to allocate more time resources to instruction and less to evaluation.

Mr. Hernandez needs to revisit the time resource balance between instruction and evaluation. He should examine how he can better include the chapter and unit tests as part of the instructional process. For example, he can return the results and discuss them as part of regular instruction. If permitted, he might have the students score their own tests, thereby gaining new insight into the content to be learned. Lastly, Mr. Hernandez needs to reexamine the purpose of chapter and unit tests. By doing so, he will realize that these tests are to be administered in a way that provides all students with an opportunity to attempt each question or respond to each item.

Supporting Documentation

Alkin, M. C., & Solomon, L. C. (1983). *The costs of evaluation.* Beverly Hills, CA: Sage.

Picus, L., & Tralli, A. (1998). *Alternative assessment programs: What are the true costs?* CSE Technical Report 441, CRESST/University of Southern California, Los Angeles.

A ACCURACY STANDARDS

Summary of the Standards

A Accuracy Standards The accuracy standards help ensure that a student evaluation will produce sound information about a student's learning and performance. Sound information leads to valid interpretations, justifiable conclusions, and appropriate follow-up. These standards are as follows:

- **A1 Validity Orientation** Student evaluations should be developed and implemented, so that interpretations made about the performance of a student are valid and not open to misinterpretation.
- **A2 Defined Expectations for Students** The performance expectations for students should be clearly defined, so that evaluation results are defensible and meaningful.
- **A3 Context Analysis** Student and contextual variables that may influence performance should be identified and considered, so that a student's performance can be validly interpreted.
- **A4 Documented Procedures** The procedures for evaluating students, both planned and actual, should be described, so that the procedures can be explained and justified.

A5 Defensible Information The adequacy of information gathered should be ensured, so that good decisions are possible and can be defended and justified.

A6 Reliable Information Evaluation procedures should be chosen or developed and implemented, so that they provide reliable information for decisions about the performance of a student.

A7 Bias Identification and Management Student evaluations should be free from bias, so that conclusions can be fair.

A8 Handling Information and Quality Control The information collected, processed, and reported about students should be systematically reviewed, corrected as appropriate, and kept secure, so that accurate judgments can be made.

A9 Analysis of Information Information collected for student evaluations should be systematically and accurately analyzed, so that the purposes of the evaluation are effectively achieved.

A10 Justified Conclusions The evaluative conclusions about student performance should be explicitly justified, so that students, their parents/guardians, and others can have confidence in them.

A11 Metaevaluation Student evaluation procedures should be examined periodically using these and other pertinent standards, so that mistakes are prevented or detected and promptly corrected, and sound student evaluation practices are developed over time.

A1 Validity Orientation

STANDARD Student evaluations should be developed and implemented, so that the interpretations made about the performance of a student are valid and not open to misinterpretation.

Overview

Explanation. Validity refers to the degree to which inferences drawn from the results of the assessment method(s) about the knowledge, skills, attitudes, and behaviors demonstrated by each student are trustworthy. Some methods that can be used in a student evaluation include the following:

- Observations
- Text- and curriculum-embedded questions and tests
- Paper-and-pencil tests
- Oral questioning
- Benchmarks or reference sets
- Interviews
- Peer assessments
- Self-assessments
- Standardized criterion-referenced tests
- Norm-referenced tests
- Performance assessments
- Writing samples
- Exhibitions
- Portfolio assessment
- Project and product assessments

Evaluators should assemble and defend the interpretations and uses of the information collected using one or more of these assessment methods. It is incorrect to say that a specific assessment method is valid. Rather, it is the inferences drawn from the information obtained from a particular method that must be valid.

To enhance the validity of inferences drawn from student evaluations, the methods for collecting information should be linked to the purposes and intended uses of the evaluation. Students should always be provided sufficient opportunity to demonstrate the knowledge, skills, attitudes, or behaviors being evaluated. Procedures for judging or scoring student performance should be consistently applied, appropriate to the assessment method used, and be regularly monitored. Procedures for summarizing and interpreting assessment results should yield accurate and informative representations of a student's performance in relation to the purpose of the evaluation. The resulting reports should be clear, accurate, and of practical value to students, their parents/guardians, and other stakeholders for whom they are intended.

Rationale. Validity is the single most important issue in student evaluation. If the evaluation is to serve its intended purpose, then the inferences and judgments made must be true and defensible. Invalid inferences or judgments can do great harm. Evaluators must take care to demonstrate to their own and others' satisfaction that they are making valid uses of information. The selection or development of assessment methods; the procedures for collecting information; and the basis for scoring, synthesizing, and drawing inferences from evaluation information must be clearly linked to the purposes for which judgments, inferences, and decisions are made. In the absence of such evidence, the inferences drawn and decisions made may be unsupportable, capricious, and harmful to a student's learning and development.

Caveats. When collecting evidence to support and defend interpretations, consider the consequences of the decisions to be made. The outcomes of some evaluations may be more critical than those of others. For example, misinterpretation of a student's level of performance could result in incorrectly holding a student from progressing to the next unit or grade, failing to recommend needed special services, or denying scholarships or even high school graduation. In such high-stakes situations, every effort should be made to ensure that evidence is available to support and defend the inferences drawn and the decisions made. Low-stakes situations can be less stringent. Regardless of the level of the stakes, evaluators should never assume that their inferences and conclusions have validity greater than what the evidence supports. Any invalid student evaluation, even if innocuous and slight, can affect a student adversely and interfere with his or her learning and development.

GUIDELINES

A. Ensure that the assessment methods used are relevant to and representative of the knowledge, skills, attitudes, or behavior identified in the purposes and uses of the evaluation (see U2, Defined Users and Uses).

B. Use more than one assessment method to substantiate findings and ensure that comprehensive and consistent indications of student performance are collected (see A5, Defensible Information).

C. Ensure that assessment instruments translated into a second language; modified to accommodate a special need or learning disability; or transferred from another context, location, or time are accompanied by evidence that the inferences obtained from these instruments are valid for the intended purpose.

D. Ensure that students understand the directions for an assessment. Provide a sample item or task where necessary to ensure understanding.

E. Ensure that interactions with students during the assessment are appropriate and consistent (e.g., while answering a paper-and-pencil test item, a student may ask to have an ambiguous term clarified. If warranted, the clarification should be explained to the entire class).

F. Restrict the number of characteristics to be observed in assessments involving observations, and ensure that they are described concretely so that the observations can be made accurately.

G. Document unanticipated circumstances that interfere with the collection of assessment information.

H. Prepare a scoring procedure to guide the process of judging a performance or product before an assessment method is used.

I. Ensure that scoring is not influenced by factors irrelevant to the performance or product being scored. Irrelevant factors include the following:
   - Stylistic factors such as vocabulary and sentence structure, when the intent is to assess content and reasoning
   - A general tendency to be too generous or too severe
   - The halo effect, where a general impression or previous rating influences the present rating
   - Environmental conditions under which the evaluation is scored (e.g., the evaluator is tired, distracted, or ill)

J. Adjust scoring procedures in light of unanticipated but appropriate responses.

K. Avoid combining disparate kinds of results into a single summary. Where possible, achievement, effort, participation, and other behaviors should be graded separately (see A10, Justified Conclusions).
L. Ensure that when the results of a series of assessments are combined into a summary comment, the actual emphasis placed on the various results matches the intended emphasis for each student (see A9, Analysis of Information).
M. Ensure that when combining the qualitative information into a summary comment and quantitative information into a summary grade, the actual emphasis placed on the information being summarized matches the intended emphasis for each student (see A9, Analysis of Information).
N. Describe and justify the basis for interpreting the information gathered for a reporting period (see A5, Defensible Information).
O. Consider the backgrounds and learning experiences of students when interpreting their performance (see P4, Treatment of Students; A3, Context Analysis).
P. Interpret assessment results taking into account limitations in the assessment methods; problems encountered in collecting, judging, or scoring the information (see A6, Reliable Information); and limitations in the basis used for interpretation.
Q. Stay abreast of new assessment methods and findings that could increase validity and reduce misinterpretations.
R. Adhere to the standards set forth in the *Standards for Educational and Psychological Testing* (American Educational Research Association, American Psychological Association, & National Council on Measurement in Education, 1999) when administering standardized tests or other standardized assessment protocols.

COMMON ERRORS

A. Using evaluation methods because of their reputation or because they have been used previously
B. Using information simply because it is available
C. Using unfamiliar assessment methods without adequate training
D. Failing to provide alternative procedures for collecting assessment information from students with learning disabilities and students whose proficiency in the language of instruction is inadequate for them to respond in the anticipated manner (see P4, Treatment of Students)
E. Using students' work samples as valid information for judging their skills without verifying that the students themselves produced the

work without inappropriate assistance (e.g., unwarranted help from parents/guardians or siblings, essays copied from the Internet or another student)

Illustrative Case 1—Description

Ms. Sorin, a third-grade teacher, was preparing a unit called Living Things and the Environment. She decided to use bats as the content for this unit. She knew that most students knew little about bats, and that many were afraid of them. To enhance the validity of what she taught and her assessments, she first identified the learning objectives for the unit. A sample of these objectives is listed below in the format that she used:

C O N C E P T S / P R O C E S S C O N C E P T S / P R O C E S S

____ Describe and compare bats according to their common characteristics, habits, and food
____ Observe the conditions necessary to produce sound
____ Use a fair test to identify any variable that causes sound
____ Develop a testable hypothesis
____ Identify the materials and procedures necessary to conduct a fair test
____ Identify the manipulated variable
____ Conduct and record an experiment
____ Make inferences and draw conclusions from test results
____ Infer the adaptive functions of bat characteristics and behaviors

Attitude

____ Demonstrate a willingness to revise views of bats
____ Develop a sensitivity and respect for bats
____ Develop an appreciation for the uniqueness of bats

Ms. Sorin used the list of objectives for four things:

- She sent the objectives home to the students' parents/guardians before beginning the unit, so that they would know what was to be taught next. As a result, one of the parents arranged for a friend to share his rather extensive bat collection with the class.
- She planned her instruction and what her students would do to acquire the knowledge, skills, and attitudes set forth in the learning objectives.

- At the same time she planned her instruction, she developed four assessment tasks, each referenced to the learning objectives, and identified where in the instructional sequence each should be administered. The first assessment was a writing piece in which the students were asked to select two species of bats, describe them, then compare and contrast them. She developed a 10-point scoring system with the students before this assignment to ensure that they understood what was expected and how grammar, spelling, and sentence structure would be graded. Next, she had the students complete an experiment on sound, which she graded using a 10-point scale that had previously been discussed with them. Third, she had the students summarize what they had learned from the presentation on bats using a 5-point grading scale she developed with the students. Fourth, she used a paper-and-pencil, end-of-unit test that included 12 multiple-choice items and two short-answer questions to test knowledge and skill, and a short-answer question to test attitude (e.g., Describe what you would say to a child who is afraid of bats so that he or she would no longer be scared).
- After she had graded the end-of-unit test, she sent the list home again, but with the students' grades (E for excellent, G for good, S for satisfactory, U for unsatisfactory) entered in the blanks to the left of each learning objective.

Illustrative Case 1—Analysis

Ms. Sorin worked to ensure that both the instruction and assessment methods were aligned with the objectives to which they were referenced. She also planned her assessments at the same time that she planned her instruction to help integrate them in meaningful ways. She used a variety of assessment methods that, when taken together, provided relevant and representative data on which to base her inferences. By involving the students in construction of the scoring guides, she helped ensure that both they and she held similar expectations. By involving the parents/guardians, she enhanced their understanding of their children's performance.

Illustrative Case 2—Description

Ms. Williams, a grade 7 science teacher in a small school located in the Bitterroot Mountains, used a variety of methods to assess the performance of her students. She then added up the scores and converted the total to letter grades. The letter grades she used were, from the highest to the lowest,

A, B, C+, C, C–, D, and F. Ms. Williams had a zero tolerance policy for absences that she announced to the students and sent home to the parents/guardians. If a student was not present for an assessment, then a score of zero was awarded. The students were not allowed to make up any missed work.

Presented here is a copy of her mark book for the January-to-April reporting period. The first 11 marks are for labs. The next three are for midterm tests and a final examination. The remaining five marks are, respectively, for attendance, care of equipment, attitude, notebook, and reading reports. The mark of A indicates absence. The marks in the bottom row are the total possible points for each component. The teacher converted the A marks to zeros, added the marks, and converted the sum to the percentages shown in the second-to-last column. The percentages were converted to the letter grades shown in the last column. The total marks for each component are shown in the last row.

No questions were raised by the students' parents/guardians when the students received their report cards. Al realized that he really did better than what the grade of D conveyed, and his mother, while not happy with the mark, understood why the mark was so low. Al's father had passed away two years earlier. On the days Al was absent, she knew that he was tending traps set to capture animals for their fur, a source of income for the family. Terri's parents were pleased with her grade. They interpreted Terri's mark of A as an indication that their daughter was a "rocket scientist."

Illustrative Case 2—Analysis

Was each student treated fairly? If the primary purpose of each reported grade is to describe a student's performance and understanding of the course concepts, the answer is no. Both Al and Terri were treated unfairly.

- Al received a 100 percent on each of the labs he completed and on the midterm test and final examination he completed. As warned by Mrs. Williams, he received no credit for the laboratory exercises that occurred on days he was absent. Also, the zero tolerance for absences spilled over to other aspects included in the teacher's grades for students. Mrs. Williams awarded him zero for attendance that, in turn, led to zero for care of equipment, notebook, and attitude, and ultimately to his grade of D for the course. However, as the grades for the labs and exams Al completed show, he had a good grasp of the material and skills to be developed.
- Terri's grade of A reflected her good attendance and subsequent high grades for care of equipment, attitude, notebook, and reading

Name	Laboratory Scores											Exams			Other					Tot. %	Gra.
Sam	6	7	6	6	5	6	6	A	7	6	7	33	39	81	15	5	7	0	0	59	C–
Pat	2	3	5	5	6	6	7	8	8	9	10	11	29	86	15	15	18	0	10	61	C
Al	10	10	A	10	10	10	A	10	A	A	10	50	A	10	0	0	0	0	15	57	D
Dan	9	8	9	8	8	9	9	9	8	9	9	26	28	56	20	14	13	20	20	70	B
Bob	10	10	9	9	8	8	7	7	6	6	5	45	34	28	20	10	15	10	5	61	C
Terri	10	10	8	10	10	10	8	10	8	8	10	23	24	46	20	20	20	20	20	72	A
Cam	8	8	8	7	9	9	8	9	10	8	8	32	30	57	20	8	7	0	0	60	C
Total	10	10	10	10	10	10	10	10	10	10	10	50	50	100	20	20	20	20	20		

Note: "A" denotes Absent in these columns.

reports, and not her performance in the lab and on the midterms and final as her parents believed. Had only factors essential to assessment of course concepts been used to grade Terri, her grade would have been substantially lower.

- Although the teacher had a zero tolerance absence policy that was known to students and parents, using that policy as a primary basis for grading corrupted the grading process. The resulting grades misrepresented students' understandings of the course concepts to parents and students. To more adequately and fairly summarize these different aspects of student performance, achievement, effort, participation, and attitude should be graded separately.

Supporting Documentation

American Educational Research Association, American Psychological Association, & National Council on Measurement in Education. (1999). *Standards for educational and psychological testing.* Washington, DC: American Educational Research Association.

Joint Advisory Committee. (1993). *Principles for fair student assessment practices for education in Canada.* Edmonton, Alberta, Canada: University of Alberta, Center for Research in Applied Measurement and Evaluation.

Joint Committee on Testing Practices. (1998). *Code of fair testing practices for education.* Washington, DC: American Psychological Association.

Linn, R. L., Baker, E. L., & Dunbar, S. B. (1991). Complex, performance-based assessment: Expectations and validation criteria. *Educational Researcher, 20*(8), 5-21.

Messick, S. (1989). Validity. In R. L. Linn (Ed.), *Educational measurement* (3rd edition; pp. 13-103). Washington, DC: American Council on Education.

Messick, S. (1994). The interplay of evidence and consequences in the validation of performance assessments. *Educational Researcher, 23*(20), 13-23.

Moss, P. A. (1994). Can there be validity without reliability? *Educational Researcher, 23*(2), 5-12.

Nettles, M. T., & Nettles, A. L. (1995). Equity and excellence in educational testing and assessment. Boston: Kluwer.

U.S. Department of Education, Office for Civil Rights. (2000). *The use of tests as part of high-stakes decision-making for students: A resource guide for educators and policy-makers.* Washington, DC: Author. Retrieved May 17, 2002, from http://www.ed.gov/offices/OCR/testing/.

A2 Defined Expectations for Students

STANDARD The performance expectations held for students should be clearly defined, so that evaluation results are defensible and meaningful.

Overview

Explanation. The teaching-learning process is based upon the expectation that students know what they are to learn and how they are to demonstrate what they have accomplished. When students, their parents/ guardians, and educators understand these expectations, they can engage in learning and evaluation processes that effectively serve the students' needs. To help provide a clear definition of the learning expectations, assessment methods should be related to the goals and objectives of instruction and be compatible with the instructional approaches used. The interpretation of the assessment results should take into account the instructional opportunities provided and the backgrounds of the students. Planning instruction and evaluation at the same time will help appropriately integrate the two (see F1, Practical Orientation). Such joint planning provides an overall perspective on the knowledge, skills, attitudes, and behaviors to be learned and evaluated, and the contexts in which learning and evaluation will occur.

Student expectations have three parts:

- Pre-specified knowledge and experience expectations—the knowledge and skills necessary to begin an instructional unit or to enter a particular program or course (e.g., unit on fractions, a high school elective, or a honors program)

- Student responsibilities within the specific educational context—the duties of students in preparing for and participating in an evaluation (e.g., what learning tasks are to be completed, when and how work is to be done, behavior during the assessment)
- Expected learning outcomes—results expected of the student. The list of expected learning outcomes could be developed from textbooks or other curricular materials, instructional notes, and additional materials used in the instructional process. Where possible, these expectations should be developed with input from students, parents/guardians, and others with a stake in student learning outcomes.

Students should be evaluated on each of these three components to ensure that the knowledge, skills, and behaviors corresponding to each component are present (e.g., whether the student has the requisite knowledge to begin a unit on multiplication, whether the student effectively participated in the instructional activities and completed required work designed to teach multiplication concepts and multiplication facts, whether the student can demonstrate knowledge of the multiplication facts he or she was expected to learn).

Rationale. Sound evaluations of students cannot be created without specifying

- What the student is to learn
- The qualifications a student should bring to the learning situation
- How the student is to act and respond in learning and evaluation situations

Failure to delineate what students are expected to learn, how they are to demonstrate what they have learned, and their responsibilities for their own learning and for demonstrating what they have learned can lead to incorrect inferences. Incorrect inferences delay or inhibit student progress and the identification of appropriate follow-up activity.

Caveats. Teachers should not use lack of knowledge of student qualifications or lack of learning opportunities to justify unexpected poor evaluation results. In most classrooms, teachers must provide learning opportunities for all students, regardless of whether the students enter fully qualified for the planned instruction. Teachers must recognize student entrance capabilities and provide learning opportunities consistent with those capabilities and what is to be learned. The educational needs of students are not served by prescribing performance objectives and related learning opportunities that students cannot meet or attain.

GUIDELINES

A. Develop expected course outcomes based on systematic analysis of the student's entry-level knowledge and skills, and the school, community, and program expectations for students.
B. Define student requirements and expected outcomes that reflect student needs; course needs (e.g., reading capability for the next level in a five-level reading program); mandated expected learning or curricular outcomes (e.g., district- and/or state-level mandated curricular objectives); and school and community requirements (e.g., graduation requirements, requirements for employment).
C. Specify in detail significant behaviors, tasks, duties, responsibilities, and performance objectives.
D. Make clear the relative importance and performance level of each standard used to define success in the course or other context being evaluated.
E. Involve students, to the extent possible, in identifying the behaviors, duties, and responsibilities to be expected of them.
F. Investigate and resolve discrepancies between stated expectations for students and the expectations to which the assessment is referenced or the criteria used to judge achievement.

COMMON ERRORS

A. Excluding relevant details from descriptions of what is expected from students
B. Evaluating the performance aspects of a course that are consistent with statewide standardized tests but are unrelated to stated course objectives
C. Failing to keep descriptions of student expectations current and accurate, so that they are aligned with actual instruction and course content emphases
D. Failing to conduct needs assessments to learn the capability and skills of entering students

Illustrative Case 1—Description

Mr. Dempsey teaches junior high school history. In addition to discussing material in the textbook, he routinely discusses current events and relates them, where applicable, to historical circumstances. He asks his students to bring to him current events they have found by reading the newspaper, listening to news on the radio, or watching television news. He told his students and their parents/guardians at the beginning of the year that his exams would cover both the material presented in the text and what he discussed in class. He explained that because, as adults, the students would be expected to independently read and discuss current events, he would include on each examination one or two items dealing with current events that he had not discussed in class.

Some of the students complained after their first exam that one of the test items did not cover information discussed in class, and that they had not studied for it. This item dealt with a recent current event that had been reported widely in the newspaper and on radio and television during the week before the exam. Mr. Dempsey included this item to see if his students were applying what they had learned in class to a new situation.

Mr. Dempsey responded to the complaints by saying that, as he had explained earlier to the students, he wanted to stretch their minds and encourage them to investigate beyond the textbook and class discussion. He also said that the additional items helped him to determine which students were sufficiently knowledgeable to receive an A for the course. In response, the students claimed that he had told them that they would be tested on textbook material and material discussed in class. He responded by pointing out that this was not all that he told them. He had pointed out he would include one or two items on new material. Once reminded of this, the students acknowledged that they thought he would not include such items, but that he did do what he said he would do, and that the failure to anticipate such items was theirs.

Illustrative Case 1—Analysis

Mr. Dempsey's inclusion of current events and their relationship to historical events is commendable. He provided guidelines for course, class, and examination content to both the students and their parents/guardians. When challenged, he was able to justify what he had done and point out to the students that they had been informed. By defining what his students were expected to learn and do, Mr. Dempsey avoided a potentially more complex and difficult situation. At the outset, Mr. Dempsey made clear his expectations that students needed to know not only the topics presented in the textbook and discussed in class, but also current events related to these topics. By including the test item, he made his evaluation consistent with his expectations for student learning.

Illustrative Case 2—Description

Mrs. North, a grade 8 mathematics teacher, has a reputation as an excellent teacher. Her students always perform well on tests and examinations. Near the end of the second semester, Mrs. North found that she did not have enough time to cover all of the material included in the unit on solving word problems. This unit covered several topic areas including interest-rate-time, distance-rate-time, income-expenses, and supply-demand. She decided that because she had covered interest-rate-time extensively in grade 7, she would omit this topic and cover the others.

The students in the class came from three different grade 7 classes, only one of which Mrs. North had taught. When the students received their marks on the problem-solving unit test, several complained about their low marks, arguing that they did not do well on the interest-rate-time questions, because this was a new topic for them and she had not covered it in class.

Knowing that she had covered this topic in grade 7, she dismissed the students' argument. She told them either to review the material on their own or attend a three-day noon-hour tutorial that she was willing to give before the final end-of-term examination. Although the students appreciated Mrs. North's willingness to give the tutorial, they were disturbed that they were expected to know something that their grade 7 teachers had not covered thoroughly and that they now had to give up their lunch hour to learn.

Illustrative Case 2—Analysis

Although Mrs. North has a well-deserved reputation as an excellent teacher, she should not have assumed that the students who took grade 7 mathematics with other teachers would have the same experiences as her students. Clearly, these students came to grade 8 math having had a different learning experience from the students she had taught in grade 7. When the students complained, she should have determined whether interest-rate-time problems were covered in all grade 7 classes and to what extent. She could have then altered their marks on the unit test to account for the differences in prior knowledge. Better still, before she made her decision to omit teaching these problems, she should have checked to see if all of the students had the same experience in solving interest-rate-time problems and adjusted her instruction accordingly. By doing so, she would have avoided the complaint raised by the students and their later disappointment.

Supporting Documentation

Banta, T., Lund, J., Black, K., & Oblander, F. (1996). *Assessment in practice: Putting principles to work on college campuses.* San Francisco: Jossey-Bass.
Lorber, M. (1956). *Objectives, methods, and evaluation for secondary teaching.* Boston: Allyn and Bacon.
Wiggins, G. (1998). *Educative assessment: Designing assessments to inform and improve student performance.* San Francisco: Jossey-Bass.
Zemelman, S., Daniels, H., & Hyde, A. (1993). *Best practice: New standards for teaching and learning in America's schools.* Portsmouth, NH: Heinemann.

A3 Context Analysis

STANDARD Student and contextual variables that influence performance should be identified and considered, so that a student's performance can be validly interpreted.

Overview

Explanation. Evaluators should identify, consider, and acknowledge the students' backgrounds, learning experiences, and temporary or extraordinary occurrences beyond the students' control that may influence performance. The results and information obtained from assessments should not be altered. However, the student, his or her parents/guardians, and other stakeholders should be helped to understand the results and information by taking into account the variables that may have influenced the student's performance.

At the student level, prior knowledge, completion of school homework, language capability, home learning environment, and learning and physical disabilities are examples of factors that influence learning. For example, poor reading ability, learning disabilities, poor test-taking skills, anxiety, and low expectations can lower performance.

At the class and school levels, poor performance may be the result of a lack of learning opportunities. If learning materials and supplies are not available, appropriate learning activities are not provided, inadequate time is designated for learning, or instruction is poor, learning opportunities may be diminished. Temporary distractions in the school should also be taken into account. For example, the school band practicing in a room below the room where an assessment is being conducted or a fire drill during the assessment will likely adversely affect the students' concentration and potentially their performance. If students miss important instruction because, for example, they attended a field trip, a student council meeting, or a funeral, the teacher should be guided by school and classroom policies for providing additional opportunities for learning and/or assessment. If alternative procedures are not feasible, the teacher should take into account these contextual factors when interpreting and reporting test scores.

Rationale. Student backgrounds and environmental factors can affect a student's performance. Interpretations of assessment results should consider these factors, so that valid interpretations and decisions can be made about each student. Ignoring such influences leads to invalid interpretations, incorrect decisions, and follow-up actions detrimental to the student. Although such factors are always important, the teacher should be especially careful to consider them when a student performs poorly.

Caveats. Sound consideration of context requires specific and known procedures for taking student background and learning experiences into account. Such consideration of contextual factors and extraneous events must not be haphazard or arbitrary.

GUIDELINES

A. Develop a written policy to guide decisions about how contextual information and extraneous influences will be accounted for in making interpretations and evaluation decisions, and make the policy available to students and parents/guardians.
B. Provide all students with a sufficient opportunity to demonstrate the knowledge they have gained or the skills they have acquired.
C. Monitor students during assessments for distractions that may influence performance (e.g., fire drill, lawnmower outside the window, disturbance in the hall outside the classroom).
D. Document and consider prior knowledge and the opportunity to learn when making evaluation decisions.
E. Record unusual or atypical behavior by individual students, and try to determine its cause before interpreting the assessment results.
F. Provide students with opportunities to explain why they think their performance was deficient.

COMMON ERRORS

A. Drawing conclusions about students' performances without taking into account the opportunities to learn
B. Ignoring the significance of students' learning experiences outside the classroom
C. Failing to consider a student's readiness to be tested
D. Failing to provide needed accommodations to students with disabilities

E. Failing to identify and consider important contextual factors (e.g., language, culture) that affect assessment results for underrepresented groups
F. Assuming that treating everyone the same eliminates the need to consider special circumstances that might affect the test performance of particular students
G. Allowing contextual information to override the real evidence of performance, so that the assessment results are ignored or distorted
H. Giving in to students who try to argue away or rationalize poor performance

Illustrative Case 1—Description

Carrie became pregnant while attending high school in a small, conservative, Midwestern town. She left school at midterm, feeling that she could not continue. In response, the school principal and Carrie's teachers looked for ways for Carrie to complete her studies at home. With the exception of biology, it was possible for Carrie to study the same material as the other students at home; hand in the same homework assignments; and take the same tests, under supervision, as the other students.

The biology class emphasized laboratory work that Carrie could not do at home. She and her biology teacher settled on an alternative way for her to earn the 40 percent laboratory portion of her grade. Instead of the labs, Carrie completed research on development of the human fetus, from conception to birth, and on the nutritional needs of a baby for the first six months of its life. She wrote a comprehensive paper and received a B for the course. With Carrie's full prior knowledge, a note indicating that the research paper took the place of the laboratory work accompanied her letter grade.

Illustrative Case 1—Analysis

In this case, the principal and Carrie's teachers took into account the context (i.e., pregnancy) of the particular student. Working together, they provided a feasible opportunity for her to complete her studies. In the case of biology, not only was Carrie given an alternative way to demonstrate what she had learned, she was provided an opportunity to submit evidence of learning within the realm of biology that fell outside the course syllabus. Reporting the letter grade along with an explanatory note provided an accurate and truthful portrayal of what the grade reflected for this student.

Illustrative Case 2—Description

Stony got his nickname because he was such a tough athletic competitor. Teachers and students both thought of him as a "jock." Stony participated little in class discussions and received average grades. However, he excelled in athletics. When he talked with his counselor about going to college, the counselor advised him to go to a junior college and possibly major in business, because his bookkeeping grades had been above average. Also, he could probably play football there.

One day, in a classroom discussion, Stony and other students shared their aspirations. Stony said that he planned to go to the local junior college and major in business. Under further questioning, it turned out that he had always secretly wanted to be an engineer, but he knew he was not "smart enough" to go to engineering school.

The classroom teacher had a higher opinion of Stony's intellect. She looked at Stony's aptitude scores in his cumulative file and found them to be exceptionally good, in contrast to his mediocre grades. His quantitative aptitude scores were above the 90th percentile on national norms. The teacher told Stony that she believed he had the potential to succeed in an engineering school. Stony did not believe her. In an attempt to convince him otherwise, and with his permission, the teacher sent the aptitude test scores and Stony's academic record to the chairman of the state university's engineering department. The chairman responded that a student with such scores would likely be accepted into engineering school, although he might need to make up some math classes.

Illustrative Case 2—Analysis

Stony had misjudged his ability to undertake a program in engineering. His grades, test scores, and even the counselor's opinion were consistent with his perception that an engineering school would not accept him. Fortunately, one of his teachers thought otherwise and looked for evidence of his academic potential. The added background information on quantitative aptitude provided different contextual information that allowed Stony to consider an alternative to junior college.

Supporting Documentation

Airasian, P. W. (1997). *Classroom assessment* (3rd edition). New York: McGraw-Hill.

Herman, J., Morris, L., & Fitz-Gibbon, C. (1987). *Evaluator's handbook*. Newbury Park, CA: Sage.

Knox, C. (1995). *Political context and program evaluation: The inextricable link.* Jordanstown, Co. Antrim, Ireland: University of Ulster.

Stiggins, R. J. (1997). *Student-centered classroom assessment* (2nd edition). Upper Saddle River, NJ: Prentice Hall.

U.S. Department of Education, Office for Civil Rights. (2000). *The use of tests as part of high-stakes decision-making for students: A resource guide for educators and policy-makers.* Washington, DC: Author. Retrieved May 17, 2002, from http://www.ed.gov/offices/OCR/testing/.

A4 Documented Procedures

STANDARD The procedures for evaluating students, both planned and actual, should be described, so that the procedures can be explained and justified.

Overview

Explanation. Documentation of both planned and actual evaluation procedures provides students, parents/guardians, and other stakeholders with a clear vision of the intended procedures to be followed and the actual procedures employed in an evaluation. The extent of this documentation is dependent on the consequences of an evaluation. As the consequences of individual evaluations increase, the need for documentation increases. Much of the teacher's evaluation of students, particularly in the early grades, focuses on student learning and feedback during the instructional process. These evaluations provide brief, timely judgments based on limited student information. Realistically, it is impossible to fully document these judgments. In contrast, more complete documentation is required for assessments such as unit tests and final examinations where the information contributes heavily to final course grades.

Rationale. In order to make sound interpretations of student evaluation results and to judge the quality of the evaluations, stakeholders must know how the evaluation was intended to be conducted and how it was actually performed. Systematic documentation of the entire evaluation process will help ensure that the evaluation will be equitable and fair. Deviations from intended procedures can produce unintentional erroneous results. The nature of any deviations must be documented and accounted for, so that the users of the evaluation can properly interpret results and avoid follow-up actions detrimental to students.

Caveats. Teachers should not jeopardize instruction time by spending unnecessary time documenting evaluations. Routine, low-stakes evaluations may have little documentation. High-stakes evaluations, where the consequences of an incorrect decision are more severe, require more careful and systematic documentation, so that stakeholders can review and assess the evaluation processes should they choose to do so.

GUIDELINES

A. Distribute information that explains the student evaluation procedures to be followed to students, parents/guardians, and other stakeholders.

B. Maintain the following information for grading and other high-stakes evaluations:
   - Course outline or syllabus, including a clear statement of evaluation purposes and procedures
   - Data or information collection plan
   - Descriptions and/or copies of the assessment methods used, including an account of how they were developed and validated
   - Descriptions of the actual procedures followed in administering the assessment methods
   - Provisions for and actual practices followed when evaluating students with disabilities
   - Dates on which assignments were given to students and when completed assignments were due
   - Guidelines for scoring assessments, including scoring keys and rubrics
   - Sample evaluations of student work (with students' names removed)
   - Guidelines for combining information to form summary comments and grades
   - Sample interim and final student evaluation reports
   - Guidelines with sample agendas for parent-teacher and student-led conferences (see U6, Effective Reporting)
   - Procedures for maintaining confidentiality of student evaluation records (see P3, Access to Evaluation Information)
   - Methods used to audit the evaluation process (see A11, Metaevaluation)

C. Collect and record systematically student and parent/guardian perceptions and judgments of the student evaluation process (see A11, Metaevaluation).

D. Address in writing any issues raised by a supervisor about a student's evaluation by referencing the record of planned and actual evaluation procedures.

COMMON ERRORS

A. Making an evaluation plan so inflexible that unanticipated events cannot be accommodated
B. Failing to note and explain deviations from intended evaluation procedures (e.g., not administering a midterm exam due to teacher illness, fire drill, unexpected school closure due to weather)
C. Changing the evaluation plan without informing students and, when necessary, parents/guardians

Illustrative Case 1—Description

Dr. Ramamoorthy, an instructor for a college English class of 100 freshmen, assigned short writing exercises throughout the semester. Because of his heavy teaching load, his three teaching assistants graded each writing assignment and the two course exams.

Professor Ramamoorthy gave grading criteria to the teaching assistants to help them grade the writing assignments. The criteria were a list of "things to look for." He also provided them with sample writings indicative of the A, B, C, D, and F grades to be assigned to the students' papers. However, the assistants were not trained in the grading process, nor were they monitored to ensure that they would arrive at grades in a uniform way. Each assistant graded some of the writing assignments and reported the grades to Professor Ramamoorthy independently. He then reported the results to the students.

Many students were baffled and unhappy with their grades. Some pointed to evidence that the papers they wrote met the scoring criteria, although they received a low grade. Others, having compared their graded papers with those of fellow students, said that they could see little consistency in how the grades were determined.

Professor Ramamoorthy was able to produce the criteria and sample answers his teaching assistants used as the basis for scoring student papers. However, he could not verify that the teaching assistants understood the grading procedures, because he had not trained them. Furthermore, he had not calibrated the grades awarded by the three teaching assistants or checked the quality and consistency of their performance. Hearing this, the students became more concerned and took the issue to the dean of the faculty.

Illustrative Case 1—Analysis

Professor Ramamoorthy erred in that he should have more fully documented the full grading process. Had he done so, it is likely that activities such as training and monitoring the teaching assistants, checking the quality and consistency of their grading, and comparing grades to ensure consistency among the graders would have occurred (see A6, Reliable Information). In the absence of these procedures, some students may have received higher scores than they should have, and others may have received lower scores than they deserved (see A1, Validity Orientation). Provided with an inadequate explanation of the grading process, some students took their concern to the dean in the form of a grievance.

Illustrative Case 2—Description

The parents of a grade 4 student asked for an appointment with the teacher, Mrs. Yenton, to discuss their son's poor grades. Their son, Jason, had received higher marks in previous years. However, Mrs. Yenton, a new fourth-grade teacher, had high learning expectations and a practice of showing her students their weaknesses as well as their strengths. At the meeting, Mrs. Yenton defended her grading of Jason in all subject areas as in his best interests. She wanted her students to aim high and to develop fully their knowledge and skills.

When the parents asked for an explanation of the evaluation process, Mrs. Yenton gave them an information sheet explaining the purposes and procedures of student evaluation for the class and walked them through its contents. She explained that all parts of the evaluation process were keyed to the goals and objectives of each subject area, and that the goals and objectives were keyed to the state's curriculum framework. She showed them her portfolio of evaluation plans, instruments, homework assignments, diagnostic charting procedures, and reporting formats.

She then turned to Jason's portfolio. By going through his portfolio with his parents, she was able to show them that Jason was being appropriately and systematically examined using assessment methods that yielded reliable and valid information. He was receiving diagnostic feedback, and was performing below the standards that he should be meeting. She shared with them more recent evidence collected since the report card that suggested that Jason was now making steady progress. The parents turned from being dissatisfied with Mrs. Yenton to asking how they could support their son's learning.

Illustrative Case 2—Analysis

Teachers should be prepared to account for the student evaluations they conduct. Students, parents/guardians, and other stakeholders have a right to know the basis for assigned grades and evaluation results (see P3, Access to Evaluation Information). When presented with clear information and justification about the student evaluation process, parents/guardians can become allies in the education process, and students are more likely to value and use evaluation results. Mrs. Yenton was able to defend her high learning standards and evaluation expectations because she had taken the time to plan, conduct, and document appropriate student evaluations that produced usable results (see U1, Constructive Orientation).

Supporting Documentation

Airasian, P. W. (1997). *Classroom assessment* (3rd ed.). New York: McGraw-Hill.

American Federation of Teachers, National Council on Measurement in Education, & National Education Association. (1990). *Standards for teacher competence in educational assessment of students.* Washington, DC: National Council on Measurement in Education.

Cangelosi, J. S. (2000). *Assessment strategies for monitoring student learning.* New York: Longman.

Linn, R. L., & Gronlund, N. E. (2000). *Measurement and assessment in teaching.* Upper Saddle River, NJ: Prentice Hall.

U.S. Department of Education, Office for Civil Rights. (2000). *The use of tests as part of high-stakes decision-making for students: A resource guide for educators and policy-makers.* Washington, DC: Author. Retrieved May 17, 2002, from http://www.ed.gov/offices/OCR/testing/.

A5 Defensible Information

STANDARD The information collected for student evaluations should be defensible, so that the information can be reliably and validly interpreted.

Overview

Explanation. Information gathered in student evaluations is the evidence for making interpretations, decisions, recommendations, and follow-up activities. As is true with any evidence, the defensibility of the information should be of prime concern. There are many ways to get adequate information to serve as the basis for student evaluations. For example, informal evaluations may be based on observations of on-task behavior, homework, group interactions, or oral reports. More formal sources include course records, test reports, report cards, and transcripts. To be defensible, the information gathered must be of such a nature and extent that it can be reliably and validly interpreted and useful to stakeholders.

Most information collected in a student's evaluation is obtained from the student. Yet data from students can be problematic or of such poor quality as to be of limited or no use. Many situations result in flawed or misleading information. Although appropriate assessment methods increase the likelihood of gathering good information, their use does not necessarily guarantee it. Even when procedures are well described and followed precisely, unexpected circumstances may result in information that is not of the quality necessary to make valid interpretations (see A1, Validity Orientation). Moreover, good procedures may result in information that is adequate for one evaluation purpose but not for another (see U2, Defined Users and Uses).

One example of indefensible evaluation information occurs when students cheat, plagiarize, or engage in other academic misconduct. A student may do another student's homework, or a student may copy information from books or the Internet. A student may have another person provide covert assistance or sit in for an exam. For these reasons, teachers should carefully monitor the students to ensure the defensibility of the information collected. Sometimes, students are asked to participate in a self- or peer assessment (e.g., in a cooperative learning group). These evaluation situations require that students are properly prepared in the assessment processes to help ensure that the ratings they provide are defensible and can be interpreted validly (see A1, Validity Orientation).

When data are obtained from people other than the students, it is important to know their qualifications and their presumed level of objectivity. Parents/guardians may be biased when they provide information used to evaluate their child. Teacher assistants may not have the content knowledge or skills to adequately judge student performance or products. Educators must be able to defend their observations and demonstrate that they are not influenced by fatigue, frustration, or other environmental factors that have nothing to do with the students' behavior or performance. For example, in an evaluation based on observation, without documentation of the misbehavior that can be defended, it is not enough to say that a child is always misbehaving.

Teachers may also be biased or confronted with conflict of interest in their evaluations of students (see P7, Conflict of Interest; A7, Bias Identification and Management). These conditions may compromise evaluation activities, especially those of an interpretive nature (e.g., scoring and judging essays or observing students during a performance assessment).

Using a variety of assessment methods helps to ensure comprehensive and consistent indications of performance and, at the same time, helps to identify any problems in the information. The separate data sources and methods serve as cross-checks for one another. When they agree, the information and evidence have been corroborated. When they yield disparate results, additional investigation should be done to learn the cause of the difference and improve the defensibility of the information.

For all types of records, steps should be taken to ensure that the data are correct and their integrity is maintained. Failure to detect biases, inaccuracies, unauthorized changes, and other problems reduces the defensibility of the data and can result in inappropriate evaluation findings and decisions (see A8, Handling Information and Quality Control).

Rationale. When teachers conscientiously use defensible information, their evaluations are more likely to serve the learning needs of their students. By monitoring and defending the quality of the information, they will increase the likelihood of making valid interpretations of student performance and recommendations of appropriate follow-up activities.

Caveats. The demands of teaching often promote the use of assessments that are expedient, rather than relevant to how their results will be used. Teachers must weigh expediency and convenience against the need for appropriate and defensible information *in guiding student development.*

GUIDELINES

A. Identify the information needed to address the purpose(s) and use(s) of the student evaluation (see U2, Defined Users and Uses).
B. Choose assessment methods and procedures that meet practical and defensible data collection constraints (see F1, Practical Orientation) while providing relevant information that can be reliably (see A6, Reliable Information) and validly (see A1, Validity Orientation) interpreted.
C. Use a variety of different assessment methods to help ensure comprehensive and consistent indications of student performance.
D. Check the type of information to be collected with other knowledgeable teachers to gain their perspectives.
E. Collect information that conforms to legal, ethical, and school-based policies for confidentiality and privacy (see P4, Treatment of Students; P5, Rights of Students).
F. Try to understand the cultural and social values of all students. Avoid topics that may be sensitive for particular groups of students unless their use can be clearly linked to the purpose and use of the evaluation (see P4, Treatment of Students).
G. Explain to students the value of accurate evidence and the negative effects of inappropriate behaviors such as cheating, plagiarism, or one student standing in for another student.
H. Keep a file or portfolio for each student containing the materials used to determine summary comments and grades. These materials may include copies of the student's work products with written teacher feedback, quiz and test scores, and anecdotal notes on the student's progress.
I. Document the reasons for the information collected and the assessment methods used. Use these records to help select and defend assessment methods and as sources for future evaluations.

COMMON ERRORS

A. Failing to gather needed information from defensible information sources (e.g., parents/guardians, counselor, other teachers) because evaluation planning occurred too late to allow the information to be collected and used

B. Choosing assessment methods and procedures based on their ease of use, rather than on their appropriateness to the questions and uses of the evaluation
C. Failing to adequately proctor or monitor an assessment (e.g., reading a book or leaving the room for extended periods while students respond)
D. Failing to ensure that unmonitored work completed outside of the classroom was done by the student without inappropriate assistance from others
E. Assuming that defensible information appropriate for one evaluation situation will also be appropriate for another evaluation

Illustrative Case 1—Description

Ms. Shriver is an elementary school teacher who is particularly conscious of the need for continuous assessment that is aligned with instruction. She strongly believes in young children's questioning and then seeking answers to their questions. She uses videotapes to document her students' "wonderings," as she calls them, and to show her students' increasing sophistication over time. Each tape is dated and labeled with information about a particular inquiry.

With the consent of their parents/guardians, Ms. Shriver displays on the classroom wall some of the students' work in the form of panels or prints from her video printer. The children's journaling or "jotting," as well as her own journaling, is also visible. Student work such as artwork, book reports, and reports about science investigations are displayed on the walls or placed on tables. Like other teachers, Ms. Shriver also uses quizzes and end-of-unit tests.

Ms. Shriver tells students about the nature of information that she intends to collect and how she will use it to help them and to talk with their parents/guardians. Students, in turn, seek her guidance in helping them to do their best. Parents/guardians come to open houses and arts and science nights and talk into tape recorders about their responses to their children's work. All of this is only some of what Ms. Shriver does to evaluate and document her students' learning.

Based on the information sources used and students' understanding of these sources, most students know and can describe what they are doing, what questions they are asking, and what they are learning. Parents/guardians who visit the classroom can see the student products and judgments and understand how Ms. Shriver arrives at the evaluative decisions made about their child. The principal, her students, and their parents/guardians rarely question the credibility or rigor of her judgments and decisions, because the information sources and the ways they are used to make evaluative decisions are clearly presented.

Illustrative Case 1—Analysis

The evaluations conducted by Ms. Shriver are based on defensible information. She operates an open evaluation process with her students, although not all of the data are open to all. She uses multiple sources and methods, informs students of these sources to guide both their instruction and preparation for evaluations, and links the evaluation sources to the evaluation decisions she makes.

Illustrative Case 2—Description

Ms. McManus is a high school ballet teacher in an urban fine arts magnet school. Students from many different parts of the city attend her ballet classes. Most have completed many years of ballet training and have arrived at the juncture of becoming serious young dancers. When it was time for Ms. McManus to audition students for a special performance class, the students were surprised at who was selected. Their parents/guardians also had difficulty understanding the selections, but admitted their own biases.

Some people felt as if the selection was based less on commitment, love of ballet, strong performance, physical strength, and grace, and more on size, height, attractiveness, parent/guardian commitment and status, and simply the teacher's preferences for certain students. When asked how she made her selections, Ms. McManus replied that she had been a dancer all of her life and had been teaching for many years. The selections were to be made by her alone, because she was the teacher. This left many students and their parents/guardians dissatisfied. Some wondered if it was worth continuing with the ballet class in the next semester given that Ms. McManus would be the teacher.

Illustrative Case 2—Analysis

Ms. McManus's failure to use defensible information in making her evaluation decisions and her failure to describe the information she did use to her students and their parents/guardians led to a loss of trust and respect. Equally important, the student evaluations did not further the students' learning or their development. Her students needed a clear understanding of what performance criteria Ms. McManus viewed as important, and why she considered these criteria significant. With this information, students would become more knowledgeable and likely work to hone skills that would enable them to grow as dancers and improve their performance. Instead, the failure to select and use defensible evaluation information likely promoted petty competitiveness, resentment among students and parents, and loss of love for ballet on the part of some students. Ms. McManus's failure to base her evaluations on adequate, defensible information could become a problem for her as dissatisfaction about her selections becomes more public.

Supporting Documentation

Cangelosi, J. S. (2000). *Assessment strategies for monitoring student learning.* New York: Longman.

Linn, R. L., & Gronlund, N. E. (2000). *Measurement and assessment in teaching.* Upper Saddle River, NJ: Prentice Hall.

A6 Reliable Information

STANDARD Evaluation procedures should be chosen or developed and implemented, so that they provide reliable information for decisions about the performance of a student.

Overview

Explanation. *Reliability* refers to the degree of consistency of the scores or information obtained from an information-gathering process. For example, would the evaluation results for a student be similar if the information was collected on one day as opposed to another day? In the case of an essay or performance task, would the scoring be the same if two different teachers marked the essay or performance? Would the students obtain the same set of scores on one form of a test (e.g., multiple-choice) as opposed to another form of the test (e.g., short answer) developed to assess the same knowledge and skills? Any time a sample of a student's work or performance is obtained for evaluation, the question of whether the information is consistent enough to be used for the intended evaluation purposes must be addressed.

Different strategies are used to assess reliability depending upon the type of data collected and the nature of the decision to be made. For example, reliability coefficients are used to describe norm-referenced decisions in which students are compared with each other. Decision consistency coefficients are used in criterion-referenced decision situations, where the performances of students are compared with a defined performance criterion. An inter-rater reliability coefficient is used when different markers score an essay, research report, product, and performance.

All assessment information contains some inconsistency attributable to factors such as ambiguous test items, mistakes in scoring, raters' differing interpretations of student performance, differences in students' attention spans, clarity of directions, and students' luck in guessing. Evaluators should determine the reliability of the assessment information or results they gather and use assessment methods that produce reliable information. They should avoid methods with poor reliability, especially when making important decisions.

As the consequences of individual evaluations increase, the need for high reliability increases. In the early grades, much teacher evaluation focuses on student learning and feedback during the instructional process. During instruction, teachers provide timely but brief judgments based on limited student information. These individual evaluative judgments are likely to have low reliability. That is, if faced with the same situation on several different occasions, the teacher's judgment or interpretation would likely differ from occasion to occasion. However, the ongoing dialogue, both individually and with the class as a whole, allows for review and correction of misperceptions. Therefore, the negative consequences of these low-reliability evaluations are likely to be small. Greater reliability is required for information sources such as final examination scores that contribute heavily to final course grades.

Rationale. All evaluation decisions are affected by the reliability of the information used. Evaluations can have major impacts on students both in their learning and in the opportunities afforded to them. Decisions of substantial consequence must rest on highly reliable results. Lesser decisions require less consistent results. Students, their parents/guardians, and other stakeholders have a right to know the levels of reliability of the information used.

Caveats. Most evaluators believe that the information on which they base their evaluations is reliable and free from error (i.e., that the reliability is near 1.0). For low-stakes decisions, this belief may be acceptable. For high-stakes decisions, reliability and decision consistency of the assessment should be documented. In high-stakes situations, using several different assessments will help to ensure consistent findings regarding student performance.

GUIDELINES

A. Determine whether the nature of the judgments and decisions to be made are norm-referenced or criterion-referenced and low-stakes or high-stakes.

B. Assess and document reliability each time an assessment method or procedure is used to ensure that the results are sufficiently consistent for the intended use.

C. Ensure that the method used to determine reliability (e.g., internal consistency, stability, observer agreement, and decision consistency) for each assessment procedure is appropriate for that method and for the interpretation to be made.

D. Use procedures to enhance reliability (e.g., increased test length, greater number of observers and scorers, use of a variety of assessments).
E. Develop high-quality instruments (e.g., tests, performance tasks, observation checklists) following accepted assessment development procedures.
F. Make the conditions of assessment as similar as possible for all students, given intended evaluation uses and taking into account individual needs and differences.
G. Ensure that procedures used for judging or scoring student performance are consistently applied and monitored.
  - Verify optical or computerized scoring by hand scoring a sample of student responses.
  - Develop protocols for scoring and judging performance assessments, including essays, to reduce inconsistencies in scoring.
  - Provide adequate training to scorers and observers to ensure that they are alert to the kinds of mistakes they are likely to make and know how to avoid those mistakes.
  - Re-score student work when it appears that the scores are less consistent than desired.
H. Check for inconsistency in interpretations of information and results among students, parents/guardians, teachers, and other stakeholders.
I. Adhere to the standards set forth in the *Standards for Educational and Psychological Testing* (American Educational Research Association, American Psychological Association, & National Council on Measurement in Education, 1999) when administering standardized tests or other standardized assessment protocols.

COMMON ERRORS

A. Assuming that information is adequately consistent when the reliability has not been determined
B. Scoring performance tasks, including essays, when tired, distracted, or inattentive
C. Assuming that the value of one type of reliability coefficient is indicative of the values of other types of reliability coefficients
D. Assuming that published values of reliability coefficients are necessarily applicable to the intended use
E. Assuming that the reliability of an assessment method or procedure is the same for different groups and situations

F. Assuming that standardized tests are reliable for all students, independent of the conditions of testing
G. Failing to take account of the lack of reliability when grading or classifying students whose scores are close to the cut scores
H. Confusing reliability with validity (see A1, Validity Orientation)
I. Assuming that adequate reliability guarantees adequate validity

Illustrative Case 1—Description

Mr. Miller prefers to base his student evaluations on a combination of in-class essay tests, short-answer mini-tests, written group work, and individual work collected in a portfolio. However, scoring all the written work is time-consuming. Mr. Miller carries student papers with him for scoring whenever he has a few free minutes and occasionally reads and scores student work during commercial breaks while watching television. Because he is so knowledgeable about the content, he usually can assign the letter grade earned by a student's responses on a test by comparing the student's papers with the ideal paper he holds in his memory. He typically reads all the answers on one student's test paper and then writes down the grade next to the student's name at the top of the page before moving on to the next student paper. After the papers of all the students have been graded, he enters the students' grades in his grade book.

Illustrative Case 1—Analysis

The reliability of the information Mr. Miller is developing, as well as the validity of the inferences he makes using this information, are threatened by his scoring procedures. Scoring the full set of items without reference to a scoring guide and scoring the student papers at various convenient times are almost certain to result in inconsistencies that will influence grades in unpredictable ways. Scoring all of the answers for one student before moving to the next may introduce "halo effects" (i.e., an impression gained about a student during instruction carries over to the scoring of essays and observing performance) and bias (see A1, Validity Orientation), while spuriously enhancing reliability.

Mr. Miller should increase the reliability of his scoring by writing out ideal answers and a scoring guide to follow in assigning points or letter grades to individual answers. He should try to score all students' answers to an individual question before moving on to the next question. In addition, he should score the answers without knowing the identities of the students by having them write their names on the back of the papers and/or shuffling the papers after each question has been marked.

Adopting these procedures has three advantages. First, Mr. Miller would be more likely to score each question more consistently, because he would be more focused and less likely to be distracted by thinking about other questions. Second, he would be more likely to complete the scoring of one answer for all students in one block of time, thereby avoiding changes brought about by different marking times. Third, by avoiding to the extent possible knowing which student's paper he is grading, the effect of personal bias toward different students can be minimized.

Whether or not Mr. Miller is concerned with the effect of extraneous events on reliability, the reliability should be checked to ensure fairness (see P4, Treatment of Students). He could do so by re-scoring a random sample of responses to selected questions and comparing the original scores to the second set of scores as an estimate of his scoring consistency. Significant deviations would indicate that he needs to create a more focused and consistent procedure for scoring student work.

Illustrative Case 2—Description

Miss Thomson usually does not believe in contests for her seventh graders, but one recently announced contest appeared to be appropriate for learning. Her students were asked to design a poster for a local charity drive. There would be prizes and public recognition for the top three posters, which she was to identify. After being told that the prizes were gift certificates that could be used to buy CDs, all the students agreed to participate.

Miss Thompson worked with the students to establish criteria to be used in the design on their posters and to judge the quality. These criteria were written on a chart, along with variations that students thought might be observed. After the students had completed their posters, Miss Thompson had to choose the three best from among the 26 produced. To ensure a fair process, she asked a colleague, Mr. Stern, to join her as a judge. She developed a scoring rubric from the criteria and expected variations and shared it with the class. After some minor changes, she and Mr. Stern talked until they came to a common understanding of what the scoring rubric meant.

On the demonstration day, Miss Thompson and Mr. Stern independently scored each poster using the scoring rubric to come up with a final score. Periodically, they checked with each other to make sure they still agreed about what the criteria meant and how these matched up with what the students actually produced. After the judging was completed, they agreed on the top two posters, but the third one gave them trouble. Miss Thompson had given one poster a very high score that Mr. Stern had scored much lower. They checked their addition of the component scores for these posters and found that Mr. Stern had made an addition mistake that, when corrected, produced a score similar to that of Miss Thompson. The combination of their scores resulted in the third winner.

Illustrative Case 2—Analysis

The poster contest was important to the students in Miss Thompson's class, and therefore the evaluation judgment was important as well. By asking a colleague to provide a second judgment and going through a careful training process, Miss Thompson improved the reliability of the judgments. Her care in preparing the rubric also increased reliability. Not only did she and Mr. Stern have something concrete to refer to while judging, but also her students knew in advance the criteria on which they would be judged. Although some students were disappointed that their posters were not selected, the students appreciated the fairness of the process and the care with which it had been implemented.

Supporting Documentation

American Educational Research Association, American Psychological Association, & National Council on Measurement in Education. (1999). *Standards for educational and psychological testing.* Washington, DC: American Educational Research Association.

American Federation of Teachers, National Council on Measurement in Education, & National Education Association. (1990). *Standards for teacher competence in educational assessment of students.* Washington, DC: National Council on Measurement in Education.

Cangelosi, J. S. (2000). *Assessment strategies for monitoring student learning.* New York: Longman.

Feld, L. S., & Brennan, R. L. (1989). Reliability. In R. L. Linn (Ed.), *Educational measurement* (3rd edition). New York: Macmillan.

Glaser, R., & Silver, E. (1994). Assessment, testing and instruction: Retrospect and prospect. *Review of Research in Education, 20.* Washington, DC: American Educational Research Association.

Linn, R. L., & Gronlund, N. E. (2000). *Measurement and assessment in teaching* (8th edition). Upper Saddle River, NJ: Prentice Hall.

U.S. Department of Education, Office for Civil Rights. (2000). *The use of tests as part of high-stakes decision-making for students: A resource guide for educators and policy-makers.* Washington, DC: Author. Retrieved May 17, 2002, from http://www.ed.gov/offices/OCR/testing/.

A7 Bias Identification and Management

STANDARD Student evaluations should be free from bias, so that conclusions can be fair.

Overview

Explanation. Bias occurs when irrelevant or arbitrary factors systematically influence interpretations and judgments made in an evaluation in a way that differentially affects the performance of an individual student or subgroups of students. There is constant potential for the intrusion of bias in student evaluations. For example, bias may arise from teachers inflating grades for favorite students, lowering grades for problem students, or acting on a preconception of what a student can or cannot do. Bias can also occur when variables are not fairly accounted for when interpreting information and data collected during an evaluation. Examples of such variables include the following:

- Cultural differences
- Language differences
- Physical, mental, and developmental disabilities
- Athletic or aesthetic prowess
- Political connections
- Gender or racial stereotyping
- Socioeconomic status.

Bias also can occur more subtly due to unfair assessment coverage. If an assessment method fails to cover important aspects of what students are expected to demonstrate (construct underrepresentation), then the meaning of the scores or information collected will be narrower than the proposed interpretation implies. Likewise, the extent to which an assessment method includes unrelated components (e.g., reading difficulty where reading is not the behavior of interest), the scores for some subgroups of students (e.g., poorer readers) will be distorted. If present, construct underrepresentation and construct irrelevance prevent valid interpretations and interfere with the formulation of meaningful or fair decisions about students.

Rationale. Bias can undermine the fairness of a student evaluation. It can distort the assessment process and corrupt judgments and decisions leading to potentially faulty follow-up to the detriment of a student. An unbiased student evaluation is one based solely on defensible criteria and sound supporting information. Evaluators should

- Recognize that bias is an ever-present threat to student evaluation
- Be vigilant and resistant to the sources of bias
- Develop a plan for identifying and addressing bias

Caveats. Evaluators must systematically look for rival explanations to account for low scores. Simply adjusting scores and grades to compensate for a low score or grade perceived to be incorrect is itself a form of bias. It is a disservice to give students false assurances that they are doing well when they are not.

GUIDELINES

A. Ensure that the procedures used to evaluate students are related to the goals and objectives of instruction and are compatible with the instructional approaches used.
B. Ensure that interactions with students are appropriate and consistent when collecting information used to evaluate students.
C. Use more than one assessment method to ensure consistent indications of student performance.
D. Develop written policy to guide the use of alternate procedures for collecting evaluation information from students with special needs and students whose proficiency in the language of instruction is inadequate for them to respond in the anticipated manner.
E. Use clear criteria and procedures for judging and scoring student performance.
F. Ensure that scoring is not influenced by factors that are not relevant to the purpose of the assessment. Examples of such factors include the following:
    - Penmanship and neatness
    - Grammatical usage when scoring essays

- Tendency to rate all students in the same way (e.g., too generously or too severely)
- Halo effects (i.e., when perceptions based on unrelated situations influence scoring of essays and other performance assessments) (see A1, Validity Orientation)

G. Consider the backgrounds and learning experiences of students when scoring student responses and interpreting the results (see P4, Treatment of Students).

H. Remove or conceal students' names before scoring student work.

I. Engage other teachers and, where appropriate, students in separately scoring essays, products, and other performance assessments, then compare the scores.

J. Summarize achievement, effort, participation, and other behaviors separately to form summary comments and grades.

K. Ensure that grades, summary comments, and recommendations are justifiable and can be defended by the evidence collected (see A5, Defensible Information; A10, Justified Conclusions).

L. Ensure that student evaluation reports are complete in their descriptions of strengths and weaknesses, promoting a balanced report (see P6, Balanced Evaluation).

M. Review and assess the evaluation process for potential sources of bias before reporting (see A11, Metaevaluation).

N. Provide a process for students and their parents/guardians to appeal a result or a report (see P4, Treatment of Students).

COMMON ERRORS

A. Failing to identify and consider one's own biases, predilections, and stereotypes when completing a student evaluation

B. Continuing to use assessment methods and procedures known to be influenced by bias

C. Employing an inflexible approach to obtaining and interpreting evaluation results irrespective of students' differing language and cultural backgrounds

D. Judging student performance based on irrelevant characteristics such as age, gender, race, religion, or other characteristics not related to the performance being evaluated (see P4, Treatment of Students; A1, Validity Orientation)

E. Ignoring or distorting certain relevant information because it conflicts with a general conclusion or recommendation (see A10, Justified Conclusions)

F. Failing to check for construct underrepresentation and construct irrelevance that, if present, will distort the results and prevent a valid interpretation
G. Basing an inference or judgment on outdated information about a student's performance

Illustrative Case 1—Description

The students in Mrs. Santos's eighth-grade history class showed a range of abilities and interests. Four students spoke and wrote English as a Second Language (ESL). At the end of a unit on the Revolutionary War, Mrs. Santos developed an assessment composed of four essay questions related to the four main issues taught in the unit. Before the test, she identified and described for the students the four criteria she would use to score their essays. The four criteria were historical content and accuracy, word choice (e.g., conveying the response in a precise and interesting way), sentence fluency (e.g., flow and rhythm of the writing), and use of conventions (e.g., showing a good grasp of standard writing conventions). Students were given 50 minutes to complete the assessment.

When scoring the essays, Mrs. Santos shuffled the students' papers before scoring each question, so there was no predictable order of whose essay was being scored for any of the questions. She scored all the responses to the first essay, then all the responses to the second essay, followed by responses to the third essay and finally the fourth essay. Although there was a range of scores on the assessment, the four ESL students scored lower than any other student on all four essays. Even though Mrs. Santos anticipated the poor performance of these students, she thought that all students should be scored in the same way using the same criteria to ensure fairness.

Illustrative Case 1—Analysis

Mrs. Santos made a number of appropriate decisions in developing and scoring the assessment. She composed essay questions to provide depth of topic coverage and provided guidelines for the expected focus and length of the responses. She randomized the order of scoring for each essay question, thus partially controlling any effect of scoring order. She completed scoring all the responses to one essay before scoring any responses to the next essay in order to maintain consistency in scoring each essay (see A6, Reliable Information).

However, Mrs. Santos also made some poor decisions that systematically influenced the interpretation of the scores of the four ESL students. The fact that the four students were not fluent in English differentiated them from the other students in the class. The weight she gave to word choice, sentence fluency, and use of conventions put these students at a considerable disadvantage relative to the native English speakers in the class. In fact, three of her four scoring criteria differentially affected ESL students. These students could have known and understood the subject matter being tested without being able to write well about it in English. The scoring criteria resulted in a bias in favor of the students whose first language is English. This does not imply that the teacher is biased or prejudiced, but that her decision to give all students the same amount of time to respond and to score using the same criteria may have led to invalid interpretations about the four ESL students' performance in history.

Mrs. Santos might have reduced the language bias by giving the four students more time to construct their responses and/or freedom to use a bilingual dictionary. If feasible, she might have assessed these students with a version of the test in their native language, particularly if evidence was available to demonstrate that the inferences drawn from the translated test were valid for the intended purpose (see A1, Validity Orientation). Alternatively, she might have provided an objectively scored test covering the same material and administered this test not only to the four ESL students but also to the remaining students to confirm their knowledge of history. Implementation of one or more of these accommodations would likely provide a more valid indication of the four students' history achievement than the procedure used.

Illustrative Case 2—Description

Mr. Stein is a college instructor teaching freshman writing on a small rural campus. About half of his students are participants in a special admissions program for inner-city students. Although these students have met regular admissions requirements, the program has a reputation around campus of bringing in low achievers.

After grading the first writing assignment, Mr. Stein noticed that most of the students from the special admissions program scored significantly lower than the class average. Recognizing a potential for bias, he made the following modifications:

- Instead of assigning writing topics as he had in the past, he gave all students the flexibility to write about topics reflecting their interests and life experiences.
- He increased his office hours to provide extra assistance and tutoring.

- Although he did not change the criteria, he reexamined his documented scoring criteria and noted that grammar and syntax carried more weight than content and clarity. This was significant given that the inner-city students tended to be weak in grammar and used different syntax from other students.

Consequently, Mr. Stein set up help sessions, offered to all students in the class, and concentrated on teaching grammar. The final grades for the course showed that although there was still some disparity, the grades of the inner-city students were more comparable to those of the other students in the class.

Illustrative Case 2—Analysis

The reputation of the program and low performance of the inner-city students could have led Mr. Stein to develop bias and give up on these students. Instead, he recognized the potential for bias, both his own and in the assessment and evaluation instruments. To combat potential bias, he modified one assessment tool and clarified another. He then provided extra assistance to address the weaknesses of the students admitted through the special admissions program. However, the assistance Mr. Stein provided in the form of alternate topics, increased office hours, and the tutorial session were offered to all of the students, so students in the special admissions program were not singled out (see U1, Constructive Orientation; P4, Treatment of Students). Perhaps more important, Mr. Stein maintained his standards for evaluation and criteria for grading and applied them equally to all students.

Supporting Documentation

American Educational Research Association, American Psychological Association, & National Council on Measurement in Education. (1999). *Standards for educational and psychological testing.* Washington, DC: American Educational Research Association.

Cole, N. S., & Moss, R. A. (1989). Bias in test use. In R. L. Linn (Ed.), *Educational measurement* (3rd edition, pp. 201-219). New York: Macmillan.

Joint Advisory Committee. (1993). *Principles of fair student assessment practices for education in Canada.* Edmonton, Alberta, Canada: University of Alberta, Centre for Research in Applied Measurement and Evaluation.

Joint Committee on Testing Practices. (1998). *Code of fair testing practices in education.* Washington, DC: American Psychological Association.

Lam, T. C. M. (1995). Fairness in performance assessment. ERIC.

Messick, S. (1989). Validity. In R. L. Linn (Ed.), *Educational measurement* (3rd edition, pp. 13-103). Washington: American Council on Education.

Reynolds, C. R. (1994). Bias in testing. In R. J. Sternberg (Ed.), *Encyclopedia of human intelligence* (pp. 175-178). New York: Macmillan.

U.S. Department of Education, Office for Civil Rights. (2000). *The use of tests as part of high-stakes decision-making for students: A resource guide for educators and policy-makers*. Washington, DC: Author. Retrieved May 17, 2002, from http://www.ed.gov/offices/OCR/testing/.

A8 Handling Information and Quality Control

STANDARD The information collected, processed, and reported about students should be systematically reviewed, corrected as appropriate, and kept secure, so that accurate judgments can be made.

Overview

Explanation. Review of student evaluation information should be conducted methodically, thoroughly, and regularly. Corrections resulting from reviews help to ensure that evaluation results will fully and appropriately serve student needs. Assessment information and evaluative judgments must be recorded and securely stored, particularly for evaluations that serve future activities such as making diagnostic decisions, formulating summary comments and course grades, and determining scholarship recipients.

Information and quality control involves determining

- What data and information will be retained
- How and where the data and information will be stored
- What procedures will be used to determine that the stored data and information are complete and correct
- How long the data and information will be stored
- What security arrangements will be needed to limit access to only those people who have a legitimate right (see P3, Access to Evaluation Information)

To facilitate their use and retrieval, stored data and information should be organized in a systematic and easily retrievable way. The manner in which the data and information are entered into a spreadsheet or computer file, student portfolio, or teacher file or mark book should be documented and verified to ensure integrity and compliance.

Rationale. Decisions based on a student's record are important and should be made with confidence that the information in the record is complete, accurately documented, systematically organized, and secure. Evaluators should periodically do a systematic review of their students' records. These reviews should focus upon when, where, how, and who assembled the information. In addition, the information for making decisions should be current, valid, and reliable. Failure of information to meet these criteria can lead to judgments and decisions that are incorrect or detrimental to the student.

Caveats. The process of establishing and maintaining student records creates possibilities for error. Evaluators may fail to adhere to systematic and verifiable procedures in order to expedite the entry of information in a student's file. Furthermore, maintaining security of data files is often assumed, but not verified, creating the potential for compromising the integrity of the files. Attention should be paid to determining what information should be placed in a student's record, who will enter the information, who will verify the entries, and how the files will be protected from unauthorized access.

GUIDELINES

A. Develop policies and procedures to ensure that evaluators are trained to carry out all of the procedural safeguards necessary to enter, retrieve, secure, and analyze information.
B. Systematically check for errors in entering, processing, and reporting recorded information. For example, use double-entry procedures (i.e., enter a student's score twice and check agreement of the two entries) and monitor the entries in students' portfolios to ensure their accuracy and completeness.
C. Use a systematic quality control process. Designated knowledgeable personnel should review policies, audit procedures for data inclusion, check on the veracity of information, verify information removal procedures, and monitor the correct use of information.
D. Routinely check with people who contribute information to a student's record to make certain the collected information is represented accurately.

COMMON ERRORS

A. Assuming that the results from test-scoring machines, computers, and other sources are accurate

B. Accepting too readily that if information is written and published, it must be accurate
C. Ignoring recommended data entry, monitoring, and distribution procedures due to time pressures or other reasons
D. Allowing unauthorized people access to privileged student information

Illustrative Case 1—Description

The office of evaluation in a large, urban school district annually administers a brief version of a nationally normed achievement test to students in the eighth grade. The purpose of the test is to determine which students will have access to the district's advanced placement program. In addition to the achievement test, classroom grades, an intelligence test, and recommendations from teachers, parents/guardians, and community members are used for advanced placement selection. The test scores and recommendations are kept in a portfolio for each student. These portfolios are stored in each school's administration office.

The criteria for admission to the advanced placement program, along with the selection process, were established by the board of education with advice from the teachers who taught the advanced placement program. Students and their parents/guardians are made aware of the cut points for the tests and how the information from the tests and recommendations are combined. Historically, 60 percent of the students who apply for admission to advanced placement are accepted based on the established criteria.

During the past year, standard scoring procedures for the nationally normed achievement test were applied. One teacher in the school recorded all the results. Based on these results, she identified 30 (25 percent) of the 120 students who took the test as meeting the advanced placement criteria in both the language arts and mathematics subtests. She then notified the parents/guardians about whether or not their child had been selected. At the same time, she sent the names of the 30 students to the counselor. Within a week of mailing the decisions to the parents/guardians, a board member called the superintendent to inquire about the results. He had received several calls from concerned parents/guardians whose children were not accepted for the advanced placement program.

The district superintendent contacted the evaluation department and requested an audit of the procedures used in managing the recent selection process, including test scores. The results of the external audit indicated that a few errors were made in scoring the language arts subtest. More importantly, the process of using multiple assessment methods had not been followed. Specifically, the intelligence test scores and recommendations from parents/guardians and community members had not been considered. Furthermore, the external audit revealed that there had been no monitoring of the scoring or any subsequent actions.

Illustrative Case 1—Analysis

Although information pertinent to the selection process was kept secure, other aspects of the evaluation procedure to identify advanced placement students were not met. The district had established a process that required that multiple types of student information collected from different sources be used in selecting students for admission to the advanced placement program. During the year in question, a teacher, who either did not know or perhaps did not accept the importance of adhering to the policy, used one of the multiple test elements, the test scores, as the only criterion for advanced placement selection, and proceeded to act on the results. Additionally, she failed to check or confirm the accuracy of her scoring. Compounding her failures, the district's policy did not include procedures for review of the teacher's computations and findings before publication of the results.

The fact that errors were made in the test scoring and that all multiple measures were not used may have been found earlier if another teacher or a supervisor in the district had conducted a routine check on the process. Interestingly, the school counselor failed to notice that the acceptance rate of 25 percent was substantially lower than the historical rate of 60 percent. Had he been more alert, he might have raised questions regarding this difference. Systematic adherence to the policy and quality control procedures likely would have eliminated the scoring mistakes and led to the inclusion of the full set of tests and recommendations, thereby improving the accuracy in selecting students for the program and increasing the comparability with previous years.

Illustrative Case 2—Description

The staff at a small junior high school decided that they would computerize their grade books, and that they would implement the new system at the beginning of the next school year. Each teacher had a classroom computer that was joined to a local school network. When the staff met to discuss this change, two concerns arose: how to maintain confidentiality of the class data file and how to ensure the integrity of the data and information entered into the computer.

To maintain confidentiality, the staff decided that a classroom teacher could enter and retrieve student data only for his or her own class. The computers were set up so that when teachers logged on to their classroom computer and entered a personal password, only their own students' data would be accessible.

Aware that students and their parents/guardians had a right to see their own information, the teachers worked with representatives of parents/guardians to develop a form to be used to access individual student data. This form was to be dated and signed by the parents/guardians making the request, dated and signed by the teacher when the data were released, and then stored in a special file located in the school office.

To address the issue of data integrity, the staff developed a computerized checklist of things the teachers needed to do when they entered data into the student file. This checklist contained the name of the data entered, the date of entry, and the date the data were verified through a double entry. These two dates could be checked against those recorded by the computer when the data were entered and verified. At the end of each grading period, a copy of the computerized checklist was placed in the file kept in the school office, creating a permanent record of data entry and maintenance that was available should any complaint be received. The teachers agreed to this procedure. To avoid loss of data due to computer failure, the data were automatically backed up on the school's server. Again, the system allowed each teacher access only to her or his own class data, thereby ensuring confidentiality and data integrity.

Illustrative Case 2—Analysis

The staff of this school were aware of how to implement a computerized grading system that would respect the need for confidentiality (see P5, Rights of Students), limit access to the data (see P3, Access to Evaluation Information), and ensure that the data were entered accurately. The system they devised appears to include appropriate monitoring procedures to ensure that the intended procedures were actually followed. However, because people often poorly protect their passwords, leave their computers on after login, and take other actions that make their files vulnerable to break-ins, additional steps should be taken to ensure integrity of data files. For example, all changes can be electronically recorded for later retrieval and verification, or changes to data can be stored in a temporary database requiring confirmation of the change on a subsequent day before finalizing the changes.

Supporting Documentation

Airasian, P. W. (1997). *Classroom assessment* (3rd edition). New York: McGraw-Hill.

Eyde, L. D., Joint Committee on Testing Practices, & American Testing Association. (1993). *Responsible test use: Case studies for assessing human behavior.* Washington, DC: American Psychological Association.

Moore, W. P. (1994). Appropriate test preparation: Can we reach a consensus? *Educational Assessment, 2*(1), 51-68.

A9 Analysis of Information

STANDARD Information collected for student evaluations should be systematically and accurately analyzed, so that the purposes of the evaluation are effectively achieved.

Overview

Explanation. Analyses of student evaluation information, when done correctly, can be used to improve instruction and effectively monitor student progress and achievement. Sound analyses help make the information collected more understandable and result in more accurate evaluation decisions. Analyses serve teachers in planning, monitoring, and modifying their teaching, as well as guiding students' progress through a unit or course. For example, analyses of a set of observations made during a group activity can help the teacher assess the effect of the group process and identify the nature and extent of participation by individual students. Similarly, analyses of the responses to the items included on a weekly quiz can be used to identify areas of weakness and strength in the class as a whole or for individual students, providing direction for further learning (see U7, Follow-Up). In addition, assessment of the results of an item/task analysis can be used to revise items/tasks and associated materials such as scoring guides, thereby improving reliability (see A6, Reliable Information) and enhancing validity (see A1, Validity Orientation).

Evaluators often will need to use both quantitative and qualitative analyses. The key distinguishing feature between quantitative and qualitative information is that the units used for analysis in quantitative information are set and standardized before collecting the information. In contrast, any use of numbers to summarize the analyses of qualitative information takes place after the information is collected and is determined by the teacher or others who are evaluating the qualitative information.

Analyses of quantitative information usually involve data collection systems where the analysis units and scoring methods are predetermined. For example, multiple-choice test items can be objectively scored. The total number correct then serves as the total score.

Qualitative analyses involve systematically compiling collected information (e.g., open-ended responses, observations, presentations) from students into categories, and then arranging the categories into interpretable themes. Analyses of qualitative information often use models or rubrics. Student essays and written or oral research reports can be judged against samples of various levels of student performance and classified accordingly. An essay can be evaluated on separate criteria related to the learning objectives of the course (e.g., originality, grammar, language use, expressed knowledge, factual accuracy). These categories can be assigned quantitative scores at this point, allowing quantitative analyses, or the interpretation may be carried out directly on the categories and themes that have been developed.

The reliability or the consistency of test or item/task scores needs to be addressed for both quantitative and qualitative analyses (see A6, Reliable Information). For quantitative analysis, attention to consistency typically focuses on the reliability of test scores (test-retest or internal consistency). For qualitative analysis, consistency typically addresses the agreement of the scores awarded either to the item/task as a whole (e.g., rubric scoring) or to components of the item/task (e.g., analytical scoring) by a single judge (intrajudge consistency) or by two or more judges (inter-judge or inter-rater consistency).

Textbooks on classroom assessment practices and the *Standards for Educational and Psychological Testing* (American Educational Research Association, American Psychological Association, & National Council on Measurement in Education, 1999) provide guidelines for sound quantitative and qualitative analysis practices. Evaluators should be aware of and follow those guidelines.

Just as analyses must meet prescribed guidelines, interpretations and judgments based on analysis results must be made within an accepted frame of reference. Typical frames of reference include the following:

- Performance in relation to prespecified content standards
- Performance in relation to peers
- Performance in relation to aptitude
- Performance in relation to expected growth
- Performance in terms of the amount of improvement or amount learned (see U5, Explicit Values)

The plan for qualitative and quantitative analyses should be developed at the time an assessment is created. When the assessment is created, criteria for making evaluative judgments are set; the purposes and evaluative judgments to be made are identified; the information to be collected is determined; and the rules for scoring, categorizing, and summarizing the information are prescribed.

Once the information has been collected and scored or sorted into categories, sound analyses usually include several additional steps. These steps may include the following:

- Creating visual displays and graphs to gain an increased understanding of how the results are distributed
- Highlighting particularly important findings for individual students and the class as a whole
- Evaluating unusual response patterns
- Selecting appropriate strategies for reporting findings to students and other stakeholders (see U6, Effective Reporting)
- Testing information quality to ensure that only sound information is used in reaching evaluation decisions

In addition to being used for constructive evaluations, analyses serve as the basis for end-of-term written comments and final marks. End-of-term analyses summarize the performance of each student across a series of evaluations completed during the reporting period. This process calls for weighting the individual results and combining them in a way that ensures that each result receives its intended emphasis in the summary comments and final marks. Also, because the end-of-term report has higher stakes for students than do day-to-day evaluations, end-of-term analyses require more comprehensive information, greater assurances of reliability and data quality, and stronger evidence of valid interpretations and conclusions.

The resulting end-of-term written comments and grades should be used together to provide a more comprehensive evaluation of a student. To be most useful, these summaries should be in accord with each other and not tell a different story or have a different emphasis.

Rationale. When performed correctly, qualitative and quantitative analysis of information can provide accurate and valid insights into an individual student's level of performance over a period of time and meaningfully guide follow-up activities. Similarly, sound analyses can provide insights into how well assessment methods are working and how they might be improved. Improper or inadequate analyses lead to distorted interpretations and incorrect decisions about student performance, providing a disservice to students and their parents/guardians.

Caveats. Evaluators should not automatically assume the superiority of either qualitative or quantitative analyses. The design of the analyses should begin when the assessment methods are being developed and should reflect the nature of the information to be collected and the evaluation questions to be addressed. Some student evaluation situations are best addressed with qualitative analyses. For other situations, quantitative analyses are best. There will also be situations where both are needed. The choice should be based on the total evaluation context including such issues as practicality (see F1, Practical Orientation), cost (see F3, Evaluation Support), and stakeholder requirements (see U2, Defined Users and Uses; A10, Justified Conclusions).

Teachers continually evaluate students. Often, these evaluations do not require the detailed operations described (e.g., judgments made during observation of student work). However, in each situation, the type of information collected and the data themselves should be defensible (see A5, Defensible Information). Correct and well-conducted analyses cannot improve the quality of the information that has been collected.

Combining scores and/or evaluation findings (e.g., in preparing end-of-term student reports) complicates the analysis process. Scores from item subsets should be combined according to a prearranged framework that reflects issues of curriculum importance and score variability. Combining different types of student performance information (e.g., achievement, effort, participation, and skills acquisition) can confound interpretation of results. In such cases, the different types of information should be analyzed and reported separately (see A1, Validity Orientation).

GUIDELINES

A. Choose an analysis that is relevant to the purpose and uses of the evaluation (see P1, Service to Students; U2, Defined Users and Uses) and to the nature of the data and information to be analyzed.

B. Ensure that the assessment process is both comprehensive (i.e., properly samples the full range of important learning objectives) and well balanced (i.e., gives appropriate weight to all identified learning objectives) (see U3, Information Scope; P6, Balanced Evaluation).

C. Prepare a scoring procedure to guide the process of judging the quality of a performance or product before the assessment method is used (see A1, Validity Orientation).

D. Before collecting the assessment information, explain to the students the criteria and performance standards to be used to score or categorize their responses.

E. Combine written and numerical summaries to provide a comprehensive evaluation of a student and add clarity to each summary.
F. Explain to students and their parents/guardians the way summaries are formulated and interpreted (see U6, Effective Reporting).
G. Base both written and numerical summaries on more than one assessment, to ensure adequate sampling of what was to be learned and to increase reliability of the summarized judgment (see A1, Validity Orientation; A6, Reliable Information).
H. Avoid combining results from measures of different constructs. Where possible, achievement, effort, participation, and other behaviors should be summarized separately (see A10, Justified Conclusions).
I. When combining subscores, use an appropriate framework for balancing curriculum importance (i.e., weighting) and consider the possible effects of score variations among the subscores.
J. Establish procedures to corroborate results of the analyses. Review results to see that they are reasonable and that qualitative and quantitative analyses used in tandem corroborate the results of each.
K. Document the analyses conducted (see A4, Documented Procedures).
L. Communicate to students the emphasis placed on each component of a summary comment or grade (e.g., intended weights for a research report, panel presentation, in-term tests, and final exam).
M. Describe and justify the basis for interpreting summary measures (see U5, Explicit Values; A10, Justified Conclusions).
N. Use visual displays to clarify the presentation and interpretation of summary results in reports and at parent-teacher conferences (see U6, Effective Reporting).
O. Use direct, plain language for written comments.
P. Use item analyses to improve the technical qualities of assessment methods and to gain insights about the students' thinking and understanding in relation to the objectives assessed (see A1, Validity Orientation; A6, Reliable Information).
Q. Maintain a record across time periods and student groups that shows the performance characteristics of individual items and tasks (e.g., standard errors of measurement, reliability, student fit indexes, item/task difficulty and fit, percentage of students who meet established criteria, reliability, revisions made).

COMMON ERRORS

A. Choosing either qualitative or quantitative analysis techniques based only on past approaches, convenience, tradition, or evaluator comfort:

- Neglecting to explore all analysis techniques available before choosing the most appropriate one
- Conducting qualitative analyses intuitively or based on preconceptions
- Conducting quantitative analyses following a recipe without understanding or paying suitable attention to the interpretational framework

B. Failing to standardize scores where the scores from the different assessments are to be weighted and added to form a numerical summary or grade

C. Using item analyses only to assess the technical quality of assessment methods and not for understanding student performance or for instructional planning

D. Failing to recognize and consider the tendency to overemphasize dramatic or unusual performance when developing written comments (see P6, Balanced Evaluation)

Illustrative Case 1—Description

Mr. Koury, the principal of a medium-sized junior high school, was concerned about the progress of his students. His concern arose from the results on statewide achievement tests administered to grade 9 students in the previous year. After receiving the scores for the school, Mr. Koury downloaded from the Internet the results of item analyses that were conducted at the state level. These analyses were not performed at the school level. However, the principal believed that if the teachers in each department met and examined the results at the state level, they might gain insights into the performance of their students, recall if they had incorrectly or incompletely taught a particular concept, and determine areas where they needed to change their instructional approach or emphasis.

With the teachers' agreement, Mr. Koury used 1½ days of the two preparation days allotted teachers at the beginning of each school year to examine the performance results of the previous year's state-mandated examinations. He asked a professor from a nearby university who taught a pre-service measurement course to provide an introduction to item analysis. The professor explained how to use the results to assess the technical quality of a test, essay, and performance assessment, and how to use them to improve understanding and instruction. The teachers then broke into their department groups, armed with a copy of the item analysis and the curriculum objectives, to complete their own analyses.

When they assembled the next day at lunchtime, the teachers felt that they had learned a lot from the item analyses. They looked at the items that were answered incorrectly by large numbers of students (item difficulty) and reviewed the incorrect alternatives that students had selected frequently (distracter analyses) in order to better understand gaps in student knowledge and pinpoint student misconceptions. They also reviewed the items that differentiated high-scoring students from low-scoring students (item discrimination indexes). Based on this review, the teachers decided that they had spent excessive time on some topics at the expense of other topics. By looking at the incorrect options, they could see how students made mistakes. They concluded by asking Mr. Koury to purchase an item analysis package with a site license so that they would be able to item analyze their own tests and gain more immediate feedback. He agreed to do so.

Illustrative Case 1—Analysis

Mr. Koury has a constructive orientation toward both his students and his teachers (see U1, Constructive Orientation). Aware of what an item analysis can do, he took steps, with the approval of the teachers, to arrange a meaningful workshop with an outside expert. It began with an introduction from the professor to how the analyses are done and then moved on to interpreting results relevant to the teachers and their students. The teachers gained a better appreciation of the need for quality assessments and how they might approach the curriculum in the coming year.

Illustrative Case 2—Description

Mr. Borges, a community college social science teacher, told his students that he would base their grade on a research position paper and a term test. He said at the beginning of the term that the research paper would count twice as much as the term test. He used this weighting to encourage the students to take a side on the issue of public versus private health care and then to defend their position based on a well-developed, well-researched argument. His term test was based on the material covered in class. This material dealt with economic issues surrounding the concept of supply and demand as related to health care. The test would have a possible score of 100 points, and the research paper a possible 200 points.

Mr. Borges told his students at the beginning of the term how they were to be graded and what was expected in the research position paper and in class. When he computed the final marks for the term, he was concerned that they might not reflect the weightings he intended and that he had explained to his students. In particular, Mr. Borges thought that the term test was having a greater influence on the term mark than anticipated. Wanting to ensure that his grading process reflected his curricular emphases and student accomplishments, he shared the marks with one of the mathematics teachers, replacing the students' names with numbers to protect confidentiality.

The mathematics teacher noted the large difference in the variability of the two sets of scores. Scores on the term test ranged from 12 to 98, whereas scores on the paper ranged from 145 to 176. That variability difference in turn influenced and confounded the weightings that Mr. Borges had intended. The math teacher addressed this problem by standardizing the scores (i.e., equating the variability of the two sets of scores) to produce the final adjusted marks shown in the fourth column in Table 1. Mr. Borges then used these adjusted marks for his grades. Neither the students nor their parents/guardians raised questions about the fairness of the total marks when they were reported.

Illustrative Case 2—Analysis

This case presents a common situation that is "resolved" through an analysis procedure to standardize scores. Standardizing scores is an equating process to make the test and position papers "equivalent." The problem arises at the close of the term, but in actuality is one that requires careful attention throughout the course, if it is to be treated appropriately. With assistance from the math teacher, the problem is identified as caused by differences in the variability of the two sets of scores (report and test).

The solution, obtained through equating (standardizing) the two sets of scores, is appropriate if certain conditions are met. Variability in scores on any assessment measure can result from differences in the ability (i.e., knowledge, skill, and accomplishments) among students and/or from the assessment process itself. Characteristics of assessments that can cause differential variability include the quality of the items, the scoring procedures employed, and the scoring scale used.

To ensure that the resulting variability is the result of differences in students' abilities, the teacher must first rule out differences that may be caused by the assessment processes. Listed in the chart on page 166 are some of the questions the teacher must answer before deciding if it is appropriate to standardize the scores.

Even when other factors similar to those identified in the chart are correct or properly addressed, weighting to serve curricular emphases must be done prudently. Here, Mr. Borges thought that he was designing the analysis to provide proper weights. However, as the math teacher saw, the analysis process he used was not fully consistent with his intentions.

Table 1 Classroom Marks

Student Number	*Term Test/100*	*Position Paper/200*	*Final Mark/300*	*Final Adjusted Mark/300*
1	12	145	157	155
2	72	168	240	238
3	98	176	272	270
4	87	170	252	250
5	74	157	231	213
6	32	154	186	186
7	41	174	215	239
8	15	150	165	169
9	66	164	230	226
10	25	153	178	181
11	82	171	253	250
12	60	167	227	231
13	91	181	272	279
14	22	152	174	191
15	35	155	190	190
16	56	160	216	210
17	47	158	205	203
18	52	162	214	215
19	14	149	163	171
20	52	175	270	266
Mean	51.6 (51.6%)	162 (81.0%)	215.5 (71.8%)	216.6 (72.2%)
Standard Deviation	28.9 (28.9%)	10.3 (5.2%)	37.5 (12.5%)	36.0 (12.0%)

Mr. Borges's intention to give double weight to the research component is thwarted by the difference in the variability of the scores for the two assessments. Measures with larger variability (in this case, the test) have a larger effect on the rank order of scores when scores are summed across measures. Consequently, the term test, with its large variability, carried more weight than Mr. Borges wanted and in actuality determined who received high final marks and who did not.

Most of the students' adjusted (standardized) scores did not differ greatly from their unadjusted scores. However, for several students, the resulting difference was substantial. For example, adjusting the scores resulted in a five-step improvement in the rank order for person 7 and a four-step downgrading for person 5. This effect on final rank order occurred because the two sets of scores (the research papers and tests) did not have equal variability. To meet Mr. Borges's stated intention to give twice the weight to the report, the standardization process was necessary.

Test	*Report*
Why was the test so variable? • Does the variability in the test correctly distinguish student abilities (knowledge, skill, and accomplishments)? • Are the students really this variable in ability, or do I have a group that is distributed in a small middle section of the ability spectrum (as the paper scores might suggest)? In that case, might the test be erroneously variable? • Are poor test items contributing to error variance? Should they be omitted from the final scores? • Are the skills documented by the test related to those on the paper, and if so, are they confirmatory and convergent?	Why are the report results so homogeneous across the students? • Did the report process adequately sample the intended abilities (knowledge, skill, and accomplishments)? • Are the students actually this homogeneous, or are there other factors at play, such as errors or biases in my scoring processes? For example, as a teacher, can I answer yes to the following questions? – Did I score each separate item for each student before going on rather than each paper from start to finish? – Did I create correct answers and/or rubrics before beginning the scoring? – Did I score these papers without knowing the identity of the students? – Was I careful to ensure the validity of the scores (e.g., not a result of student cheating)? – Are these scores reliable estimates of student ability?

Although Mr. Borges reported no complaints from students, such changes are not likely to be uniformly appreciated, especially if students believe the final score will be the result of a simple summing process. As the example above shows, the "equate before you weight" process lowers the final standing of some students. Although the equating process improves validity (see A1, Validity Orientation), as a matter of political viability (see F2, Political Viability), clarity in student expectations (see A2, Defined Expectations for Students), and documented procedures (see A4, Documented Procedures), the equating procedures should have been explained to students at the beginning of the term.

Illustrative Case 3—Description

An art education professor, Ms. Vogel, required that her 15 student interns, who were student teaching in various K-12 urban and suburban public schools, create a portfolio that she would use to evaluate their student teaching. Seventy-five percent of each student intern's grade for student teaching would be based on the evidence of his or her students' work as contained in the portfolio. The remaining 25 percent was based equally on the intern's performance on an end-of-term paper-pencil test of art education methods and their participation in the student teaching seminars.

Before they began student teaching, Ms. Vogel told the interns to include in their portfolios evidence of their students' growth and development during the semester. She said that she would be the sole evaluator of the portfolios, which were due at the last meeting of their student teaching seminar. Given the number of portfolios she would have to evaluate, Ms. Vogel said that the portfolios should include only one sample of a few students' work, and that these work samples could be in any medium (crayon, watercolor, clay, etc.) that the students had used during a specific instructional activity. No information was provided about how the interns were to select the samples of work to include in their portfolios. Consequently, the student work samples were from a single art project that the intern had conducted, and only the work of a few students was to be included in the portfolio as representative of the intern's semester-long practicum.

Ms. Vogel assigned a rating of excellent, average, or poor to the entire assemblage of art products that a student intern submitted. These ratings were based on her expert judgment of typical artistic attainments of students at the grade level taught by each intern.

After the semester, student interns picked up their portfolios and compared their grades. Most interns received grades of A or B. Several of the interns who received grades of C or C minus complained to the department head that the evaluation was unfair, citing the fact that it was conducted in a way that was too subjective and open to bias.

Illustrative Case 3—Analysis

The student interns were justified in their dissatisfaction with the evaluation process. First, it was inappropriate to base most of the interns' grades on their students' attainments without systematically evaluating the student teachers' instructional skills. Second, the rating applied to the students' artwork was based on a narrow sample of student work products, not the products of all of the students in the class or classes that the interns taught.

Third, the inclusion of only one sample of artwork by a student precluded an assessment of student growth and development initially called for by the professor. Fourth, the grading process failed to consider that student art aptitude levels might have varied considerably across the different groups of students with different backgrounds. Fifth, only the professor rated the work products, which introduced the possibility that her own biases would influence the grading. Sixth, the professor provided no rubric or other mechanism to guide her evaluations of student portfolios, thereby reducing the reliability of her grading process and the richness of feedback provided to students.

The validity of the evaluation process would have been enhanced if the interns had been graded, in part, on their instructional skills, rather than relying so heavily on the single, qualitative rating of the student work products chosen for inclusion in the portfolios. Ms. Vogel could have systematically collected observation information on the student interns while they were teaching and on the schools and classroom contexts in which the interns taught. This would have supplemented her knowledge of the student interns' capabilities beyond what was documented in the portfolios.

It would also have been desirable to collect student work samples representing several art projects, permitting a more reliable and valid judgment of the quality of work being produced by the students under the direction of the interns. In addition, provisions should have been made to guarantee that student work samples were not plagiarized or otherwise improved unfairly by the student teachers or students' parents or siblings. Having a set of categories for the assessment of the student work would have helped both Ms. Vogel and her student interns understand the criteria upon which the evaluation was to be based. In addition, having the student interns or another art educator independently evaluate the portfolios would have reduced the potential for bias present when only one person completes an evaluation. Such changes would have ensured that the grades given to the student interns were credible, verifiable, and warranted.

Illustrative Case 4—Description

Mr. Cheng, a grade 9 English teacher, developed a unit that required students to write for different purposes and different audiences. The activities included writing a set of instructions similar to those found in a manual, a letter to the editor, and a résumé. Mr. Cheng worked with the students to develop specific criteria for each writing assignment. He designed various learning activities with the specific criteria attached, so that the students understood the relationships between purpose, audience, and form of writing.

The unit covered the entire reporting period. To complete an evaluation of the three writing projects, Mr. Cheng used the criteria he developed with the students and the school's performance letter grade scale. This scale consisted of seven values:

A The student demonstrates excellent or outstanding performance in relation to the expected learning outcomes for the course or subject and grade.

B The student demonstrates very good performance in relation to the expected learning outcomes for the course or subject and grade.

C+ The student demonstrates good performance in relation to the expected learning outcomes for the course or subject and grade.

C The student demonstrates satisfactory performance in relation to the expected learning outcomes for the course or subject and grade.

C– The student demonstrates minimally acceptable performance in relation to the expected learning outcomes for the course or subject and grade.

IP In progress. The student is making progress, but additional time is required to reach the expected learning outcomes for the course or subject and grade. Expectations and time lines must be attached for each assigned IP.

F Failed or Failing. The student has not demonstrated, or is not demonstrating, minimally acceptable performance in relation to the expected learning outcomes for the course or subject and grade. F (Failed) may be assigned only if an IP (In Progress) has not been previously assigned.

For example, a particular student, Paul,

- completed the writing of instructions, meeting the six criteria for writing good instructions, and demonstrated a B on the school's performance scale
- completed the letter to the editor, meeting five of the eight criteria for the activity, and demonstrated C performance on the school scale
- completed the résumé, meeting six of the nine criteria, but missed an important component and therefore demonstrated a C performance on the school scale.

Mr. Cheng entered comments on each piece of writing to explain the grade the student received.

At the end of the term, Mr. Cheng reviewed the three evaluations and determined a final term grade. He determined that Paul's performance was meeting all the criteria at a reasonably high level. He assigned a C+, the letter grade with the description that best matched Paul's performance. He then added the following comments on the report card to enhance the meaning of the letter grade:

> Paul's progress in writing is above expectations for his grade level. He is able to write instructions similar to those found in the user manual for a stove, refrigerator, or television. He can write a letter to the editor that conveys the essence of the message he wishes to communicate and a résumé to be used when searching for a job. Paul needs to be more careful to include all the elements needed in each of the forms of writing. The sentences he writes tend to be short and simple. He needs to work on using a greater variety of sentence structures. Paul's spelling is still a little weaker than what it should be. During the next term, the class will be working on sentence structure, and hopefully this will encourage Paul to add variety to his writing.

Mr. Cheng's comments helped the students to understand their final grades and what they meant. They knew what they needed to do to improve their performance during the next grading period. Parents who requested conferences said that the grading system was clear to them. Conference time could be spent discussing what they could do at home to help their children learn and achieve better in the future.

Illustrative Case 4—Analysis

Mr. Cheng worked to capture the essence of each student's work within the school's reporting policy that letter grades must be reported for each subject. Working with his students, he developed criteria that they could use in their writing and that he could use to judge their papers. His determination of final grades appears to have been fairly subjective and open to bias, because no information was provided as to how he arrived at his overall finding of excellent, very good, good, etc., for each student. However, he did provide substantive and helpful comments on each student's report card, based on individual assessment processes. Those comments provided the students with insights into the bases for their grades.

Supporting Documentation

Airasian, P. W. (1997). *Classroom assessment* (3rd ed.). New York: McGraw-Hill.

Coffey, A., & Atkinson, P. (1996). *Making sense of qualitative data: Complementary research strategies.* Thousand Oaks, CA: Sage.

Ebel, R. L., & Frisbie, D. A. (1991). *Essentials of educational measurement* (5th ed.). Englewood Cliffs, NJ: Prentice Hall.

Frechtling, J., & Sharp, L. (Eds.). (1997, August). *User-friendly handbook for mixed method evaluations*. Washington, DC: Division of Research, Evaluation, and Communication, Directorate for Education and Human Resources, National Science Foundation.

Glass, G. V, & Hopkins, K. D. (1996). *Statistical methods in education and psychology* (3rd edition). Boston, MA: Allyn and Bacon.

Marzano, R. J., Pickering, D., & McTighe, J. (1993). *Assessing student outcomes: Performance assessment using the dimensions of learning*. Alexandria, VA: Association for Supervision and Curriculum Development.

Miles, M. B., & Huberman, A. M. (1994). *Qualitative data analysis: An expanded sourcebook* (2nd ed.). Thousand Oaks, CA: Sage.

O'Connor, K. (1999). *The mindful school: How to grade for learning*. Arlington Heights, IL: Skylight Training and Publishing.

Perrone, V. (Ed.). (1991). *Expanding student assessment*. Alexandria, VA: Association for Supervision and Curriculum Development.

Stiggins, R. J. (1997). *Student-centered classroom assessment* (2nd ed.). Upper Saddle River, NJ: Prentice Hall.

A10 Justified Conclusions

STANDARD The evaluative conclusions about student performance should be explicitly justified, so that students, their parents/guardians, and others can have confidence in them.

Overview

Explanation. Evaluators should plan, conduct, and present student evaluations in ways that lead to justifiable and understandable conclusions. They should work from clear evaluation purposes, questions, and pertinent information. Their methods should be logically and technically sound. Evaluators should be prepared to share their evaluation plans, procedures, findings, and supporting rationale with students, parents/guardians, and other stakeholders. If it becomes necessary to deviate from publicly stated plans to reach judgments, evaluators should inform students and other stakeholders of the deviation and both explain and justify the action. Where possible, conclusions should be accompanied by a discussion of plausible alternative explanations of the findings and why these explanations were rejected.

Rationale. The important consequences of student evaluations argue strongly for ensuring that the decisions are justified appropriately and made accessible to all stakeholders. This justification is important in ensuring the acceptability of evaluation findings and decisions. The acceptability of resulting actions or educational decisions is heavily dependent on the adequacy of the data and information collected; procedures employed to collect and analyze data and information; and persuasiveness of the logical, theoretical, and empirical rationales supporting the conclusions.

Caveats. Although teachers should exercise care in reaching justifiable evaluative conclusions, they should not be overzealous in documenting and justifying every evaluative action, because this will take time away from instruction and interaction with students. Many of a teacher's evaluations occur in a dynamic classroom setting. To maintain a smooth, functional flow of instruction and evaluative feedback, it is almost impossible for teachers to explicitly justify all evaluative judgments. This limitation does not exempt teachers from the requirement that all student evaluations be conducted in ways that will enable such justification in situations when it is requested and appropriate.

GUIDELINES

A. Develop a written framework to guide student evaluations, including student learning objectives, content breakdowns, needed performance information, sources of evidence, guides for analyzing data and information, and guides for making interpretations and drawing conclusions.
B. Ensure that classroom evaluation plans are consistent with the school's instructional and evaluation policies, and periodically review them in staff meetings.
C. Make available to students and other stakeholders the objectives of student evaluation(s) and the general evaluation plan. This documentation should be presented in language that can be understood by all stakeholders.
D. Inform students why an assessment is being conducted and how the information collected will be used.
E. Provide students with sample questions and answers, including scoring guides and rubrics, to assist them in understanding the assessment.
F. Illustrate for students how summary comments and grades are formulated and interpreted.
G. Maintain evaluation materials for review by stakeholders.

COMMON ERRORS

A. Failing to recognize and take into account limitations in the assessment methods used; problems encountered in collecting, judging or scoring the information; and difficulties in interpretation when formulating conclusions
B. Stating conclusions or citing evaluation findings to justify recommendations when the available assessment data and information are insufficient or too narrow in scope to support those conclusions
C. Using an authority base, such as, "because I am the teacher, and I make the rules," "when you have taught as long as I have, you

just know," or "I know good work when I see it," rather than providing a straightforward explanation or reason for evaluative judgments

D. Presenting new reasons for a prior judgment as a means to quell a student's questions or objections

Illustrative Case 1—Description

Parents of Jana, a third-grade student, attended the fall parent-teacher conference that was tied to the first reporting period of the school year. Following a brief discussion of general school activities, attention turned to Jana's performance during the fall term, with the teacher pointing to a portfolio of Jana's work. This was the first grade in which Jana had received a letter grade for each course. The teacher briefly described Jana as active, attentive, and a willing worker who was getting along well in the school generally and in each of the courses for which grades were assigned.

Although these comments indicated that Jana was progressing in a positive way, there were differences among Jana's grades for the various courses (e.g., reading and mathematics). Wanting to know more about the variations in Jana's performance in different subjects, her parents asked for a better understanding of the grades and the grading process. Although many student work products were available for review, the teacher did not describe his grading procedures or use samples of Jana's work to clarify his grading decisions. Instead, he said, "When you have taught as long as I have, you just get a feel for these things." Not wanting to antagonize the teacher, the parents dropped the matter, but left the meeting uncertain about the school's learning environment and the teacher's fairness.

Illustrative Case 1—Analysis

Although student work products were available to Jana's parents and the teacher was prepared to give his overall judgments, he could not describe the evaluation process, his assessment procedures, or the evaluative criteria he used. Any questions about the process evoked an authority-based response from the teacher.

The failure of the teacher to describe his evaluation procedures prevented the parents from understanding why Jana received different grades in different courses. Her teacher's comments discouraged the parents' involvement in the instruction and learning process and provided no means for them to give Jana direction in how to be fully successful in class.

Illustrative Case 2—Description

Dr. Binal, a university graduate school professor, developed a Web-based course in statistics. Students from all over the world could enroll and complete the course via computer and correspondence. They obtained the instructional materials and worked through them at home. They received evaluations of their performance via e-mail, based on the instructor's assessments of the materials they submitted.

The university awarded the students "virtual credit" based on the professor's assessments of tests taken on-line and the materials they submitted. The intent of the virtual credit was to inform each student of the extent to which he or she had satisfied the course requirements and achieved the learning objectives. The virtual credit certificate clearly stated that the university assumed, without verification, that the student alone had done the work, and that the virtual credit was intended solely for feedback to the student. Virtual credit could be converted to actual university credit only if the student went to the university and passed a two-hour oral examination and a two-hour proctored written examination.

One student who had received an A grade of virtual credit and then had it validated via the on-site examinations stated this information in his job application for a position as a statistician. The job search committee informed this candidate that credit via computer and correspondence courses was not acceptable, because someone else could have done his coursework.

After receiving this information, the student contacted his statistics professor for assistance. The professor sent the search committee the statistics course prospectus, the grading criteria used in the statistics course, the university's evaluation policies for awarding actual credit, a description of the particular on-site evaluation that had been administered, and a copy of the institution's certification that the student had met the requirements for an A in the course. The search committee accepted the validity of the work the student had done in the on-line statistics course, hired him, and later found him to be an excellent statistician.

Illustrative Case 2—Analysis

Professor Binal's ability to justify the student's grade in the on-line statistics course was important to the student, the employer, and the university. The student's course achievement was validated. The employer received information that met his concerns about this particular distance education course and as a result got an excellent employee. The university successfully defended the credibility of its distance education statistics course and its grading policies and practices.

Supporting Documentation

Airasian, P. W. (1997). *Classroom assessment* (3rd edition). St. Louis: McGraw-Hill.

Airasian, P. W., & Gullickson, A. R. (1995). *Teacher self-evaluation tool kit*. Thousand Oaks, CA: Corwin.

American Educational Research Association, American Psychological Association, & National Council on Measurement in Education. (1999). *Standards for educational and psychological testing.* Washington, DC: American Educational Research Association.

Joint Committee on Standards for Educational Evaluation. (1994). *The program evaluation standards.* Thousand Oaks, CA: Sage.

A11 Metaevaluation

STANDARD Student evaluation procedures should be examined periodically using these and other pertinent standards, so that mistakes are prevented or detected and promptly corrected, and sound student evaluation practices are developed over time.

Overview

Explanation. Sound student evaluations can appropriately guide decisions and future actions designed to further the educational development of students. Flawed student evaluations can lead to incorrect decisions and actions that impede or harm students. Consequently, student evaluations themselves should be reviewed and evaluated.

A metaevaluation is an evaluation of an evaluation. The overarching question to be addressed in a metaevaluation of a student evaluation is, Are the inferences made from the information and data collected valid and not open to misinterpretation? More specific questions that might be addressed include the following:

- Have the students been appropriately informed about the purposes and nature of the evaluation?
- Is the assessment method clearly related to the instructional objectives in proportion to their importance, and compatible with the instructional approaches used?
- As administered, is the assessment method appropriate for all students?
- Has the evaluation been designed and conducted according to sound measurement principles so that inferences based on the results are reliable?

- Are evaluation reports understandable and useful?
- Is evaluation feedback timely and helpful?
- Are students' privacy and other rights maintained?

Evaluators should create and sustain the expectation that their student evaluations will be judged against the standards presented in this book, as well as other professional and state standards. These metaevaluations should be systematically planned and conducted. The results of metaevaluations should be used to address problem areas and increase the effectiveness and fairness of student evaluations.

Rationale. Student evaluation is difficult to do well, and it is subject to mistakes and complaints. Student evaluations must be scrutinized regularly to ensure that they are producing fair and accurate information that is useful for the specified purposes. Failure to evaluate and ensure the quality of student evaluations may lead to incorrect follow-up actions that may be harmful to students. Complaints need to be investigated to ensure fairness, avoid expensive appeals and litigation, and identify components of the evaluation that need to be revised.

Caveats. Metaevaluations are often difficult to plan and conduct because of competing and more pressing instructional needs. Despite this, evaluators should make a reasonable effort to assess their own student evaluation practices. The effort devoted to a metaevaluation will vary with the complexity of the student evaluations and the importance of the decisions to be made.

GUIDELINES

A. Involve students, parents/guardians, and other stakeholders in the metaevaluation.
B. Investigate whether student evaluation has had a positive effect on the educational development of the students.
C. Compare the way in which the evaluation was conducted with the way in which the evaluation was planned.
D. Judge the extent to which the evaluation purposes, plans, and procedures met the standards in this document and other relevant standards.
E. Identify parts of student evaluations that require more frequent review or closer monitoring.
F. Maintain a list of individuals who are competent to participate in designing and conducting metaevaluations, and, when feasible, engage an external person to assist in the metaevaluation.

COMMON ERRORS

A. Ignoring metaevaluation findings or otherwise failing to make needed revisions
B. Waiting to review and examine an evaluation until complaints are received
C. Assuming that a student evaluation practice is basic and stable, so that metaevaluation is not needed
D. Rationalizing that metaevaluations cannot be done because of limited time and resources
E. Relying too heavily on marginally qualified individuals to conduct the metaevaluation (e.g., using other teachers who are not trained in measurement or evaluation)
F. Making metaevaluation judgments in the absence of evidence

Illustrative Case 1—Description

Several parents/guardians complained to the North Ridge High School principal that their children had received unfair grades in a chemistry class. They claimed that their children had worked hard in the course, had completed the homework on time, and, in their view, had learned much. However, their children were given D and F grades, and the teacher, Mr. Robertson, would not explain or justify the grades to the students or their parents/guardians.

The principal assured the parents/guardians that student evaluation was an important part of the instructional process and that each teacher was expected to exercise the utmost professionalism in assessing student achievement. He acknowledged the parents/guardians' concerns and promised to investigate.

The principal then met with Mr. Robertson, summarized the parents' complaints, and asked for an explanation. Mr. Robertson was defensive, asserting his prerogative to assign grades using his experience and judgment and not explain how he assigned grades to anyone. Rejecting this line of reasoning, the principal provided the teacher with a copy of *The Student Evaluation Standards*. He then gave Mr. Robertson a week to deliver a report describing and assessing the extent to which his student evaluation practices during the past term had met or failed to meet acceptable student evaluation practice.

Mr. Robertson reviewed *The Student Evaluation Standards* and the school assessment policies. Based on what he learned, he reexamined his student evaluation practices. His report noted that he had failed to provide students with a written explanation of the student evaluation criteria and process, failed to give interim feedback during the course, not shown students the basis for their letter grades, not derived grades solely from students' tests or work products, and denied the students an avenue for appeal. He agreed to recompute the grades for his students based only on the students' work products and test results, and to provide each student with a written explanation of the grade, including reference to explicit grading criteria and each student's performance record. In addition, Mr. Robertson agreed to prepare a student evaluation plan for the next term's course and to show the steps being taken to meet *The Student Evaluation Standards*.

The principal reviewed and approved the revised grades, the written explanations, and the teacher's new evaluation plan. The principal and Mr. Robertson then met with the concerned parents/guardians and their children, reported the results of the review process, and described the student evaluation plan for the next term.

Illustrative Case 1—Analysis

Mr. Robertson should have based his students' grades on their tests and work products and used clear, defensible grading criteria. He should have explained the evaluation rationale and process to the students in advance. The principal correctly challenged Mr. Robertson in a private meeting. He provided the teacher with a meaningful framework for self-assessment and an analysis of what he had done and what he might have done. The possible bias of Mr. Robertson's own self-designed self-assessment was offset by the use of *The Student Evaluation Standards* and the principal's review of what he proposed to do in response to what he uncovered in his self-assessment. Fairness and respect were served by reconstructing and correcting the students' grades (see P4, Treatment of Students). Directly and professionally addressing the grievance and examining the student evaluation process via accepted standards averted a potential escalation of parents' hostility toward the school and the teacher.

Illustrative Case 2—Description

Professor Cohen had 14 graduate students in his measurement and evaluation class. One student had both a vision and a hearing problem. He had lost one eye, had limited vision in the other, and had an 80 percent hearing loss in both ears. Concerned with how he should evaluate this student while at the same time maintaining the standards expected of advanced graduate study, and aware of *The Student Evaluation Standards*, Professor Cohen met with the director of the Specialized Support and Disability Services (SSDS) at the university. Together with the student, Professor Cohen and the director developed a strategy that would allow the student to take the midterm and final examinations along with the rest of the students. Using equipment from the SSDS unit, the printed form for these two examinations could be enlarged and printed in bold, enabling the student to read the examination more easily. With these adjustments, the student would then be able to write in the same room as the other 13 students, but with the need for additional time.

Professor Cohen presented the strategy to the chair of the department and a colleague in measurement and evaluation. They were asked to ensure that the proposed strategy would allow an equitable assessment of the special-needs student's learning, while at the same time being fair for the other students in the class. Once both they and the special-needs student approved the plan, Professor Cohen presented the plan to the other students in the class and explained why special arrangements were needed. The students were asked if they had any questions or concerns.

After Professor Cohen marked the examinations and computed the final grades, he asked his colleague and the department chair to review his marking system, his final grades, and how he had arrived at the final grades. In particular, he asked them to ensure that no bias had entered into the process of awarding grades.

After receiving their final grades, several students came to Professor Cohen and commented on the respect and fairness of the entire process. They thanked him for taking the time to involve all of the students in a discussion of the plan and said this had been a valuable learning experience for them.

Illustrative Case 2—Analysis

Professor Cohen clearly expected that his student evaluations would be evaluated. Furthermore, he was aware of *The Student Evaluation Standards*. Consequently, he was prepared to subject his evaluations to a metaevaluation by his colleague and department chair.

Professor Cohen took concrete steps to ensure that both the student with the special needs and the other students in the class were treated with equity, fairness, and respect (see P4, Treatment of Students). He sought and accepted expert advice. He involved the special-needs student in developing a plan for taking the same examinations as the other students. With that student's permission (see P5, Rights of Students), he involved the other students by informing them of the procedures to be followed and inviting them to voice any concerns. To ensure comparability of procedures across all students, he asked a colleague knowledgeable in the content area and the department chair to comment on his plan and to review his marking, formation of grades, and how the grades were determined. Clearly, the process was of instructional value to all the students. Reference to *The Student Evaluation Standards* and willingness to have his evaluation procedures metaevaluated both before and after the student evaluations provided a foundation for an equitable and fair evaluation of all students.

Supporting Documentation

American Educational Research Association, American Psychological Association, & National Council on Measurement in Education. (1999). *Standards for educational and psychological testing.* Washington, DC: American Educational Research Association.

Joint Advisory Committee. (1993). *Principles for fair student assessment practices for education in Canada.* Edmonton, Alberta, Canada: University of Alberta, Centre for Research in Applied Measurement and Evaluation.

Joint Committee on Testing Practices. (1998). *Code of fair testing practices in education.* Washington, DC: American Psychological Association.

Joint Committee on Testing Practices. (1999). *Test takers' rights and responsibilities.* Washington, DC: American Psychological Association.

National Education Association. (1992). *NEA Handbook: Ethical standards to teachers' relations with pupils.* Washington, DC: Author.

Sanders, J. R., & Nafziger, D. H. (1977). *A basis for determining the adequacy of evaluation designs.* Occasional Paper Series, No. 6. Kalamazoo, MI: Western Michigan University Evaluation Center.

Scriven, M. S. (1969, February). An introduction to meta-evaluation. *Educational Products Report, 2*(5), 36-38.

Shadish, W. R., Newman, D. L., Scheirer, M. A., & Wye, C. (1995). Guiding principles for evaluators. *New Directions for Program Evaluation, 66.*

Stufflebeam, D. L. (1974). *Meta-evaluation.* Occasional Paper Series, No. 3. Kalamazoo, MI: Western Michigan University Evaluation Center.

Stufflebeam, D. L. (2000). The methodology of metaevaluation as reflected in metaevaluations by the Western Michigan University Evaluation Center. *Journal of Personnel Evaluation in Education, 14*(1), 95-125.

U.S. Department of Education, Office for Civil Rights. (2000). *The use of tests as part of high-stakes decision-making for students: A resource guide for educators and policy-makers.* Washington, DC: Author. Retrieved May 17, 2002, from http://www.ed.gov/offices/OCR/testing/.

Resource A: The Support Groups

PROJECT OFFICERS

The following persons reviewed proposals and reports and provided general administrative liaison between the W. K. Kellogg Foundation and the project:

Rosana G. Rodriques
John Seita

PROJECT STAFF

Staff members at the Western Michigan University Evaluation Center who wrote drafts of the *Standards*, coordinated its review and field-testing, and carried out other daily project activities included the following:

Jennifer Fager
Dale Farland
Arlen Gullickson
James Sanders

VALIDATION PANEL

The validation panel was appointed as an oversight committee to monitor the process and outcomes of the *Standards*. The responsibilities of this panel included analysis of assumptions underlying the project, critique and report of the Joint Committee's validation process, assessment of the applicability of *The Student Evaluation Standards*, identification of issues and ideas related to the development of the *Standards*, and a public assessment of *The Student Evaluation Standards*.

Two members, W. Todd Rogers, panel chair, and Daniel Stufflebeam, panel member, served two years at the beginning of the process. At the request of the Joint Committee Chair, they resigned from the panel to assist in the writing of these standards.

Chair

W. Todd Rogers (1997-1999), University of Alberta, Canada
Robert Linn (1999-2002), University of Colorado

Members

Kathleen Boundy, Center for Law and Education
J. Placido Garcia, Jr., Albuquerque, New Mexico
Douglas E. Harris, The Center for Curriculum Renewal
Audrey M. Kleinsasser, University of Wyoming
Daniel Stufflebeam (1997-1999), Western Michigan University
Victor L. Willson, Texas A & M University

PANEL OF WRITERS

Alternative versions of the standards statements were written by the following individuals.

National Panel of Writers

Max Arinder, Legislative PEER Committee, MS
Rose Baker, PA
Karen Banks, Wake County Public Schools, NC
Fred Bartelheim, University of Northern Colorado
Debbie Bass, SC
Peter Behuniak, Connecticut State Department of Education
Jeri Benson, University of Georgia
Bianca Bernstein, Arizona State University
Susan M. Brookhart, WV
Colin Burke, MD
Edith Cisneros-Cohernour, University of Illinois, Champaign-Urbana
Gregory Cizek, University of Toledo

Barbara Clements, Evaluation Software Publishing, VA
Alice Corkill, NV
Melissa Dark, Purdue University
Deanna De'Liberto, D2 Assessments, Inc., NJ
Sylvia Dean, Evergreen School District, WA
Sandy Enger, The University of Alabama, Huntsville
Robert P. Fox, MA
Lynda Green, Director of Curriculum, CT
Michael Harmon, Georgia Department of Education
John Hattie, University of North Carolina, Greensboro
Roland C. Haun, KY
Andrew Hayes, University of North Carolina at Wilmington
Joan Herman, University of California–Los Angeles
Arthur Hernandez, University of Texas–San Antonio
Craig Hilmer, San Antonio Urban Systemic Initiative
Dennis J. Hoban, Wake Forest University
Mary Huba, Iowa State University
James C. Impara, University of Nebraska
Eva Kampits, NAESC, MA
Theo R. Levernez, KY
Alvin Lubov, IL
Henry St. Maurice, University of Wisconsin–Stevens Point
Kim McDougal, Office of Program Policy Analysis and Government Accountability, FL
Kim Metcalf, Indiana University
William Moore, Ewing Marion Kauffman Foundation, MO
Dale Mueller, CA
John Nash, University of Texas–El Paso
Lori Nebelsick-Gullett, Richardson ISD, TX
Phyllis Clemens Noda, Satellite of the University of Wisconsin, MI
John Olson, American Institutes for Research, DC
Lisa L. Osen, Aevi Vision, WI
Rionda Osman-Jouchoux, CO
Dale Pietrzak, Kent State University
Jianping Shen, Western Michigan University
Barbara S. Plake, University of Nebraska
Marcy Reisetter, South Dakota State University
Edward Roeber, Council of Chief State School Officers
Lawrence R. Rogien, Boise State University
Katherine Ryan, Head, University of Illinois
Maurice Scharton, Illinois State University
Anuradhaa Shastri, College of Oneonta, SUNY

Keith Steinhurst, Central Texas College District
Richard Stiggins, Assessment Training Institute, OR
Julie Stoffels, Western Michigan University
Sherry Sullivan, University of Wisconsin
David Summers, Office of Program Policy Analysis and Government Accountability, FL
James R. Swanson, Sr., FL
Diane Swartz, Western Michigan University
Norman Webb, University of Wisconsin–Madison
Terri Wenzlaff, Western State College
Dale Whittington, John Caroll University
Diane Wilen, Multicultural/Foreign Language ESOL Education Department, FL
Teri Wing, MT
Carl A. Woloszyk, Western Michigan University
Steven Wong, CA
Mary E. Yakimowski, Hampton City Schools, VA
Nancy Zajano, Legislative Office of Education Oversight, OH

International Panel of Writers

John Anderson, University of Victoria, Canada
Marjorie Clegg, Ontario, Canada
Elizabeth Jordan, University of British Columbia, Canada
Joan Kruger, SIAST-Program Research and Development, Saskatchewan, Canada
Randy Randhawa, University of Saskatchewan, Canada
Lyn Shulhn, Owens University at Kingston, Ontario, Canada
Alan Taylor, Applied Research and Evaluation Services, British Columbia, Canada

CONSULTANTS

Specialized project functions, including serving on special writing task forces and chairing small group work sessions, were performed by the following persons.

Gwen Airasian, Elementary teacher, Newton, MA
Peter Airasian, Boston College
Edith Beatty, CESS, University of Vermont
Joan Farland, Elementary teacher, Vermillion, SD
Todd Frauenholtz, Mathematics teacher, Lauderdale, MN

Geneva Haertel, SRI International, CA
Norris Harms, Curriculum and test development specialist and farmer, CO
Frances Lawrenz, University of Minnesota
Bernard McKenna, National Education Association–retired
Todd Rogers, University of Alberta, Canada
Rick Stiggins, Assessment Training Institute, OR
Daniel Stufflebeam, Western Michigan University
Robert Wilson, Queens College, Canada
Donald Yarbrough, University of Iowa

NATIONAL REVIEW PANEL

The first draft of *The Student Evaluation Standards* was critiqued by the following persons:

Sally Adkin, North Carolina School of Science & Mathematics
Peter Airasian, Boston College
William Barratt, Indiana State University
Richard Benjamin, Cobb County Schools, Marietta, GA
Rajika Bhandari, MPR Associates, Inc., CA
Yvonne Bigos, FL
Kathy Bonn, University of North Dakota
Ronald Bonnstetter, University of Nebraska
Kathryn Borman, University of South Florida
Gretchen Boyer, AZ
Bruce Bracken, The College of William & Mary
Flora Caruthers, The Office of Program Policy Analysis and Government Accountability, FL
Eric Crane, New Education Options, CA
James R. Crites, Western Michigan University
Daniel Daste, TX
Kelly Deaver, Jefferson County Public Schools, KY
Kathleen Del Monte, University of South Florida
Dena Dossett
Dan Eignor, Educational Testing Service, NJ
Howard Evertson, NY
Betty Ferris, Jefferson County Public Schools, KY
Mark Figueroa, The Mona Group LLC, CA
Jane Fletcher, FL
Maria C. Fortino, Western Michigan University
Len Foster, University of Montana

David Frisbie, The University of Iowa
Jo Gallagher, Florida International University
Jo-Ann Gerde, Gardner Public Schools, MA
Alan Ginsburg, DC
Ed Haertel, Stanford University
Carine Strebel Halpern, University of Central Florida
Matthew J. Haring, Western Michigan University
Steve Harkreader, Stanford University
Dianne Henderson, CTB/McGraw Hill, CA
Steve Henry, KS
Michael Herrick, WI
Michael Hughes, Emory University
W. Jay Hughes, Georgia Southern University
Emily D. Jackson, Western Michigan University
Erin K. Janda, Western Michigan University
Brenda A. Katz, MI
Phil Kelly, Boise State University
Ken Kelsey, MN
Lorie Leak, MI
Mary Lieker, MI
Phil Lineroad, Northside Independent School District, TX
Teri A. Loher, MI
Kathleen Mackin, CLL University System of New Hampshire
Max Martin, Edgewood School District, TX
Mike McCoy, UT
Judy L. Mcgowan, MI
David P. Meengs, Western Michigan University
Holly Miller, Professional Data Analysts, Inc., MN
Robert Moore, MD
Rachael Moreno, MI
Michael E. Myers, Western Michigan University
Howard Mzumara, Indiana University–Purdue University
Anton Netusil, Iowa State University
Winifred Nweke, GA
Thomas Oakland, University of Florida
Olatunde Ogunyemi, Grambling State University
Scott Olsen
Les Omotani, IA
Lynde Paule, Educational Consultant, Portland, OR
Carole Perlman, IL
Marcia Perry, NH
Gary Phillips, DC
Sonja Poole, CA

Diana Pullin, Boston College
A.M. Srikanta Rao, Tuskegee University
Liesel Ritchie, Mississippi State University
Barbara Sandall, Western Illinois University
Ramsay Selden, American Institutes for Research, Washington, DC
Lorrie Shepard, University of Colorado
Joyce Sibbett, Westminister College
Susan Smith
Paula I. Steffens, Western Michigan University
Michelle L. Strang, Western Michigan University
Laura A. Sytsma, Western Michigan University
Jerome Thayer, Andrews University
Alice Thomas, MN
Kallen Tsikalas, Center for Children & Technology, EDC, New York, NY
Barbara Turnbull, Rutgers University
James Uphoff, OH
Herbert Walberg, University of Illinois, Chicago Circle
Jennifer L. Wielinga, Western Michigan University
Christine M. Wilkins, MI
John Wright, AZ
Suzanne M. Ziehl, MI
Rebecca Zittle, University of New Mexico
Rebecca Zulli, University of North Carolina

INTERNATIONAL REVIEW PANEL

Colleen Adams, Edmonton Public Schools, Canada
Ray Adams, Edmonton Public Schools, Canada
J. Dale Armstrong, University of Alberta, Canada
Lorna Earl, University of Toronto, Canada
Carl Nishimira, Edmonton Public Schools, Canada
Maria Vakola, England
Robert Wilson, Queens College, Canada

PARTICIPANTS IN THE FIELD TEST

The following individuals applied the semifinal draft of the *Standards* to various classroom student evaluation situations and reported their judgments and recommendations:

Jennifer Aldrich, Allegan Public Schools, MI
Gail Blowe, Johnston County Schools, NC
Melinda Jo Bohan, Marcellus Community Schools, MI

Melissa Borghorst, Deland High School, FL
Tricia Bridges, Petal School District, MS
Eric Brown, Johnston County Schools, NC
Sharon Brunson, Mobile County Schools, AL
Libby Carpenter, Glenn High School, NC
Mary Kathleen Christian, Gull Lake Community Schools, MI
Marianne Cingalia, Rowan University
Sarah Cooley, Madison County Schools, NC
Maggie Coxon, Oconee County School District, SC
Leslie Creek, Asheboro City Schools, NC
Scott Crocker, Portage Northern High School, MI
Ilene Davis, Poplarville High School, MS
Hope DeVenney, Lowndes County Schools, MS
Donna Dowdy, Asheboro City Schools, NC
Sonya Corbin Dwyer, University of Regina
Pamela Ehly, Iowa City Community School District, IA
Rhonda France, Three Rivers Community Schools, MI
Amy Frauenholtz, Luther Seminary, MN
Todd Frauenholtz, University of Minnesota
Angela Garcia-Sims, InterAmerican College, CA
Michael Gillen, Lincoln International Studies School, MI
Linda Gillespie, Lowndes County Schools, MS
Bruce Gillett, Osceola County Schools, FL
Clara Gilmer, Lowndes County Schools, MS
Dana Greenburg, Osceola County Schools, FL
Jean Gullickson, Michigan State University
Karen Gullickson, Western Michigan University
Pam Haga, Asheboro City Schools, NC
P. J. Hallam, Center for Language and Learning, CA
Maye Harrison, Lowndes County Schools, MS
Eva Hendrix, Mobile County Schools, AL
Mary Hess, Luther Seminary, MN
Marnie Horn, Edmond Public Schools, OK
Zechariah Hoyt, Niles Community School, MI
Jeanne Hubelbank, Wheaton College Filene Center, MA
J. Anne Hunter, Woodward School for Technology and Research, MI
Gwen Keith, Regina Catholic Schools, Saskatchewan
Cyril Kesten, University of Regina, Saskatchewan
Laurie Knight, Mobile County Schools, AL
Elizabeth Kutzli, Olivet Community Schools, MI
Debra LaFountaine, Osceola County Schools, FL
Linda Lee, Manitoba

Sandy Lee, Florida State University School, FL
Chandra Manning, Asheboro City Schools, NC
Lisa Martin, Oconee County School District, SC
Dutchess Maye, J. H. Rose High School, NC
Joyce McNair, Wilson County Schools, NC
Danny McPherson, Columbus County Schools, NC
Gale Mentzer, The University of Toledo, OH
Gillen Michael, MI
Mary Miller, Poplarville High School, MS
Ronnie Miller, George County Schools, MS
Kristine Minner, Polk County Schools, FL
Heather Minsker, Florida State University School, FL
Jayne Mohr, Traverse City Area Public Schools, MI
Linda Morrell, University of California, Berkeley
Bridget Morton, West Shore Jr. High School, FL
Scott Muri, Osceola County Schools, FL
Kathleen Norris, Gulf High School, FL
Anne Nower, Parchment Middle School, MI
Midge Ogletree, Columbia High School, NC
Maria Ostiguin, Lincoln International Studies School, MI
M. Owens, Hudson High School, FL
Seth Parker, Three Rivers Community Schools, MI
Kimberly Parker-DeVauld, Kalamazoo Public Schools, MI
Jeffrey Powless, Paw Paw High School, MI
P.L. Preston, Polk County High School, NC
Sherron Prewitt, Burke County Public Schools, NC
Carol Query, New Hanover County Schools, NC
Courtney Rakocy, Quincy Middle School, MI
Cheryl Renneckar, Gulf High School, FL
Linda Ridout, Johnston County Schools, NC
Bruce Rogers, University of Northern Iowa
Kimberly Rushton, New Hanover County Schools, NC
Diane Rutledge, Johnston County Schools, NC
Kim Ryals, North Forrest High School, MS
Ann Schultheis, National Heritage Academies, MI
Kelli Self, Asheville City Schools, NC
Roberta Sessions, Charlotte-Mecklenberg Schools, NC
Patty Spruile, Columbia High School, NC
Debbie Stanley, Hoke County School District, NC
Claudia Thompson, Northeastern High School, NC
Terris Todd, Battle Creek Public Schools, MI
Robert Wallace, New Orleans Center for Science and Mathematics, LA

Sopfia Ward, Tarboro High School, NC
Kiersten Whiting, Osceola County Schools, FL
Gail Williams, Guilford County Schools, NC
Mark Winters, Effingham County Schools, GA
Teresa Yancey, Florida State University School, FL
Andrea Zommers, St. Mary School, MI

Analysis and reporting of the field test results were supported by a grant from the Iowa Measurement Research Foundation to Donald Yarbrough. Three graduate students provided assistance with the analysis and reporting.

Susan L. Cheuvront, College of Education, University of Iowa
Jerri Drummond, College of Education, University of Iowa
Eric J. Vanden Berk, College of Education, University of Iowa

PARTICIPANTS IN THE NATIONAL HEARINGS

The following persons provided formal testimony in the national hearings on the *Standards*.

Bill Auty, Oregon Department of Education
Eric Vanden Berk, University of Iowa
Marcie Bober, San Diego State University
Wesley D. Bruce, III, Indiana Department of Education
Jennifer Coyne Cassada, Fairfax County Public Schools, VA
Mitch Chester, Ohio Department of Education
Marianne Cinaglia, Rowan University
H. Gary Cook, Wisconsin Department of Public Instruction
Julie Dunstan, Bermuda Ministry of Education
Lorna M. Earl, Ontario Institute for Studies in Education
Reed Early, Canada
Paula Egelson, SERVE Regional Educational Laboratory, NC
Louis Fabrizio, North Carolina Department of Public Instruction
Mark Fetler, California Department of Education
David Frisbie, The University of Iowa
Diane Giner, Prince Edward Island Department of Education
Peter R. Grant, University of Saskatchewan
Marilyan Hébert, University of Calgary
Jeanne Hubelbank, Wheaton College
Robert Johnson, University of South Carolina
Philip P. Kelly, Boise State University

June Koster, Rockingham County Schools, NC
Anne Kraetzer, Kraetzer Whiteneck Research
Morris Lai, University of Hawaii
David Lloyd, Nunaut Department of Education
Linda Mabry, Washington State University, Vancouver
Horace "Brud" Maxcy, Maine Department of Education
Wendy McColskey, SERVE Regional Educational Laboratory, NC
Barbara McCoy, Greenville Public Schools, MS
Joyce McNair, Wilson County Schools, NC
Stephen F. Mello, University of California–Santa Cruz
Ronald E. Mertz, St. Louis Public Schools
Noreen Michael, Virgin Islands Department of Education
Stephanie Mowry, Prince Edward Island Provincial Treasury
Georgetta Myhlhousen-Leak, William Penn University
Larisa M Naples, LMN Evaluations
Steve Nelson, Northwest Regional Educational Laboratory
Dianna Newman, State University of New York at Albany
Cornelia Orr, Florida Department of Education
Tania Rempert, Youth Guidance
Sue Rigney, U.S. Department of Education
Judy Robbins, Mississippi Department of Education
Kelly Rodgers-Sturgeon, New Brunswick Department of Training & Employment
Glenn Rowley, Victorian Curriculum and Assessment Authority, Australia
Craig Russon, W. K. Kellogg Foundation
Alan Ryan, University of Saskatchewan
Hal Sanderson, Utah Office of Education
Monika Schaffner, Bowling Green State University
Charles Thomas, George Mason University
Sally Tiel, Idaho Department of Education
Leslie Vaala, Lethbridge College
Stanley Varnhagen, University of Alberta
Tom Williams, Granville County Schools, NC

CLERICAL ASSISTANCE

Most of the word processing and clerical assistance was provided by the following persons:

Brian Carnell
Christine Hummel

Jean Poppe
Mary Ramlow
Barbara Wygant

EDITORIAL ASSISTANCE

Sally Veeder, Western Michigan University, edited the first and second drafts in preparation for the review panels and the field test.

Tish Davidson, consultant, completed a technical edit of the final draft to improve readability of the standards for teacher and lay audiences.

Resource B: Checklist for Applying the Standards

The Student Evaluation Standards guided the development of this (check one):

_____ Student evaluation plan/design/proposal
_____ Review and analysis of student evaluation practices
_____ Evaluation report
_____ Other

To interpret the information provided on this form, the reader needs to refer to the full text of the *Standards*.

The *Standards* were consulted and used as indicated in the table below (rate as appropriate):

The standard was **M**et	**M**	The standard was **N**ot met	**N**
The standard was **P**artially met	**P**	The standard was **N**ot **A**pplicable	**NA**

Standard	*Rating*	*Comments*
***P** Propriety Standards*		
P1 Service to Students		
P2 Appropriate Policies and Procedures		
P3 Access to Evaluation Information		

P4 Treatment of Students		
P5 Rights of Students		
P6 Balanced Evaluation		
P7 Conflict of Interest		
***U** Utility Standards*		
U1 Constructive Orientation		
U2 Defined Users and Uses		
U3 Information Scope		
U4 Evaluator Qualifications		
U5 Explicit Values		
U6 Effective Reporting		
U7 Follow-Up		
***F** Feasibility Standards*		
F1 Practical Orientation		
F2 Political Viability		
F3 Evaluation Support		
***A** Accuracy Standards*		
A1 Validity Orientation		
A2 Defined Expectations for Students		
A3 Context Analysis		
A4 Documented Procedures		

A5 Defensible Information		
A6 Reliable Information		
A7 Bias Identification and Management		
A8 Handling Information and Quality Control		
A9 Analysis of Information		
A10 Justified Conclusions		
A11 Metaevaluation		

Name: ______________________________ Date: ____________________
(typed)

Signature: ____

Position or Title: ______________________________________

Agency: ____

Address: ____

Relation to Document (e.g., author of document, evaluation team leader, external auditor, internal auditor) ______________________________

____

____

____

____

____

Glossary

The terms in this glossary are defined as they are used in this volume, in the context of student evaluation. In other settings, a number of them may have different or less specialized definitions.

Accuracy The extent to which an evaluation conveys technically adequate information about the performance and qualifications of a student.

Achievement What a student has learned as a result of formal instruction, usually in school.

Achievement test Assessment method, usually in paper-and-pencil format, designed to measure student competency or acquired knowledge, skills, attitude, or behavior in relation to specified learner expectations.

Analytic scoring The use of a scoring key containing an ideal response to judge the competence or proficiency of student responses on an assessment.

Anecdotal record A short, written report of an individual's behavior in a specific situation or circumstance.

Anonymity (provision for) A situation in which it is not possible to identify an individual.

Appropriate user A person who has a legitimate right or the consent of a student and, if necessary, the student's parents/guardians to see the results and findings of the evaluation of the student.

Aptitude A student's capability or potential for performing a particular task or skill.

Assessment The process of collecting information about a student to aid in decision making about the progress and development of the student.

Assessment method A strategy or technique evaluators may use to acquire evaluation information. These include, but are not limited to, observations, text- and curriculum-embedded questions and tests, paper-and-pencil tests, oral questioning, benchmarks or reference sets, interviews, peer and self-assessments, standardized criterion-referenced and norm-referenced tests, performance assessments, writing samples, exhibits, portfolio assessment, and project and product assessments.

Audiences Those persons to be guided by the results of student evaluations in making decisions about the development and progress of students and all others with an interest in the evaluation results and findings.

Audit (of an evaluation) An independent examination and verification of the quality of an evaluation plan, the adequacy of its implementation, the accuracy of results, and the validity of conclusions.

Authentic assessment Method of assessment in which the student is expected to demonstrate his or her competence and proficiency through the completion of a task that mimics a job or a higher educational or life skill.

Behavior Specific, observable actions of a student in response to internal and external stimuli.

Benefit An advantageous consequence of a program or action.

Bias A constant error; any systematic influence—on measures or on statistical results—irrelevant to the purpose of the evaluation.

Checklist A list of performance criteria for a particular activity or product on which an observer marks the student's performance on each criterion using a scale that has only two points (e.g., present or absent, adequate or inadequate).

Competency A skill, knowledge, or experience that is suitable or sufficient for a specified purpose.

Conclusions (of an evaluation) The final judgments and recommendations resulting from the assessment information collected about a student.

Confidentiality (provision for) Situation in which the identity of students will not be released to other individuals or institutions beyond the teacher or others who evaluate students.

Conflict of interest A situation in which an evaluator's private interests affect her or his evaluative actions, or in which the evaluative actions might affect private interests.

Construct A characteristic or trait of individuals inferred from empirical evidence (e.g., numerical ability).

Construct irrelevance Occurs when the assessment used to measure an educational or psychological construct includes items or measures that are not relevant (extraneous) to the construct and cause scores to be different from what they should be.

Construct underrepresentation Occurs when some of the aspects that represent the construct to be addressed are not included in the assessment used to measure it.

Context The set of circumstances or acts that surrounds and may affect a particular student, learning situation, classroom, or school.

Contextual variables Indicators or dimensions that are useful in describing the facts or circumstances that surround a particular learning situation and influence a student's performance in that situation.

Correlation The degree to which two or more sets of measurements vary together; e.g., a positive correlation exists when high values on one scale are associated with high values on another; a negative correlation exists when high values on one scale are associated with low values on another.

Credibility Believability or confidence by virtue of being trustworthy and possessing pertinent knowledge, skills, and experience.

Criterion-referenced Performance interpreted in relation to prespecified standards.

Critical score A specified point in a predictor distribution of scores below which candidates are rejected or considered not to have reached a minimum standard of performance; also called a cut score.

Cross validation The application of a scoring system or set of weights empirically derived in one sample to a different sample drawn from the same population to investigate the stability of relationships based on the original weights.

Curriculum The knowledge, skills, attitudes, behaviors, and values students are expected to learn from schooling; includes statement of expected student outcomes, descriptions of material and activities, and the planned sequence that will be used to help students acquire the expected outcomes.

Data Evidence, in either numerical or narrative form, gathered during the course of an evaluation and that serves as the basis for information, discussion, and inference.

Data access Conditions under which access to information is provided, including who has the access.

Data analysis The process of organizing, summarizing, and interpreting numerical, narrative, or artifact data, so that the results can be validly interpreted and used to guide future development of students.

Data collection procedures The set of steps used to obtain quantitative or qualitative information about the knowledge, skills, attitudes, or behaviors possessed by a student.

Decision consistency coefficient Like the reliability coefficient, this is a calculated value that tells the extent to which the decision results (e.g., classifications) would be the same if the process were repeated. It is often used in either-or decision situations (e.g., mastery-nonmastery). Like the reliability coefficient, a coefficient of zero (0) means no consistency and a coefficient of one (1.0) means fully consistent.

Dependability A measure of how consistent the results obtained in an assessment are in a criterion-referenced evaluation; consistency of decisions in relation to prespecified standards (see Reliability).

Design (evaluation) A representation of the set of decisions that determines how a student evaluation is to be conducted; e.g., identifying purposes and use of the information, developing or selecting assessment methods, collecting assessment information, judging and scoring student performance, summarizing and interpreting results, reporting evaluation findings, and following up evaluation results.

Diagnosis Identification of specific strengths and weaknesses in a student's learning.

Discrimination index An index that indicates how well an item distinguishes between the students who understand the content being assessed and those who do not. Positive discrimination indicates that the item or task is discriminating in the same way as the assessment method of which it is a part.

Educational objective A statement describing the knowledge, skill, attitude, or behavior a student is expected to learn or perform and the content on which it will be performed as a result of instruction.

Evaluation Systematic investigation of the worth or merit of a student's performance in relation to a set of learner expectations or standards of performance.

Evaluator Anyone who accepts and executes responsibility for planning, conducting, and reporting student evaluations.

External evaluation An evaluation conducted by an evaluator from outside the classroom.

Feasibility The extent to which an evaluation is appropriate and practical for implementation.

Follow-up Actions taken to maintain the strengths and address the weaknesses that were identified in the evaluation of the student.

Formative evaluation Evaluation conducted while a creative process is under way, designed and used to promote growth and improvement in a student's performance or in a program's development.

Grading system The process by which a teacher arrives at the symbol, number, or narrative presentation that is used to represent a student's achievement in a content or learning area.

High-stakes evaluations Evaluations that lead to decisions that, if incorrect, harm students and are detrimental to their future progress and development. For example, misinterpretation of the level of performance of an end-of-unit test may result in incorrectly holding a student from progressing to the next instructional unit in a continuous progress situation. Every effort should be made in high-stakes evaluations to ensure that the assessment method will yield reliable and valid results.

Holistic scoring Method of scoring essays, products, and performances in which a single score is given to represent the overall quality of the essay, product, or performance without reference to particular dimensions (see Analytic scoring).

Informed consent Prior to the collection of this information and/or its release in evaluation reports, an agreement by students—and, if the students are of minority age, their parents/guardians—that their names and/or the confidential information supplied by them may be used in specified ways, for stated purposes, and in light of possible consequences.

Instruction The methods and processes used by teachers to change what students know and can do, their attitudes, or their behavior.

Instructional objectives More detailed expressions of educational objectives (see Educational objective).

Instrument An assessment device adopted, adapted, or constructed for the purposes of the evaluation.

Inter-rater coefficients This is a special type of reliability coefficient used to determine the extent to which two or more raters are consistent in their scoring of students. It is often used to determine whether two judges grade in the same way (e.g., would students receive the same grade if their responses were graded by two different teachers).

Item A single question, problem, or task used to assess a student (see Task).

Item analysis A technique employed to analyze student responses to objective test items. The technique is used both to improve the quality of items and to enhance interpretation of results. This technique shows the difficulty of the items and the extent to which each item properly discriminates between high-achieving and low-achieving students.

Learner expectations or outcomes See Instructional objectives.

Letter grade A summary evaluation of a student's proficiency or competency expressed on an alphanumeric or numeric scale.

Low-stakes evaluations Evaluations that lead to decisions that, if incorrect, are less harmful to students and likely will not interfere with their progress and development. For example, incorrectly completing an in-class assignment is less harmful than failing an end-of-unit test in a continuous progress situation.

Mandated assessments Assessments teachers are required to conduct to fulfill the duties associated with their terms of employment, such as assessments for grading and promoting students and assessments required by district or state policy (district and state assessments).

Mean The arithmetic average of a set of numbers.

Measurement The process of assigning numbers or categories to performance according to specified rules.

Metaevaluation An evaluation of an evaluation.

Norms A set of scores that describes the performance of a specific population of students at a particular grade level on a selection or constructed response set of tasks. The population may be a local, state, or national population. These sets are used to interpret scores of students on the same selection or constructed response set of tasks and belonging to the same population.

Objective scoring Different scorers or raters will independently arrive at the same score or ratings for a student's performance; most often associated with assessment methods comprised of selection items (see Subjective scoring).

Options Alternatives available to students to select from in multiple-choice items.

Parallel forms Two or more forms of a test constructed to be as comparable and interchangeable as possible in their content, difficulty, length, and administration procedures and in the scores and test properties (e.g., means, variance, and standard error of measurement).

Peer assessment An assessment method in which students within a similar educational setting make and report judgments about other students' performances.

Performance assessment A formal assessment method in which a student's skill in carrying out an activity and producing a product is observed and judged (e.g., construction of a woodworking project; completion of an essay in English, research report in history, or lab in science).

Performance criteria The observable aspects of a performance or product that are observed and judged in a performance assessment.

Performance standards The levels of achievement students must reach to receive particular grades or to be allowed to move to the next unit in a criterion-referenced assessment system (e.g., 90 percent and higher receive an A, between 80 percent and 89 percent receive a B, and so on; a student who receives a score of 80 percent or more moves on to the next unit, while retained students need to review the material tested and retake the test or a parallel form of it).

Pilot test A brief, simplified preliminary trial study designed to learn whether a proposed evaluation seems likely to yield valuable results.

Portfolio assessment Method of assessment that relies on a collection of student- and/or teacher-selected samples of student work or performance in order to evaluate individual student achievement.

Propriety The extent to which an evaluation will be conducted legally, ethically, and with due regard for the welfare of those involved in the evaluation as well as those affected by its results.

Qualitative information Information presented and/or summarized in narrative form, for example, written expressions descriptive of a behavior or product.

Quantitative information Information presented and/or summarized in numerical form; for example, scores on a paper-and-pencil test or on a five-point analytical scale.

Random sampling Drawing a number of individuals from a larger group or population, so that all individuals in the population have the same chance of being selected.

Reliability A measure of how consistent the results obtained in an assessment are in a norm-referenced evaluation situation; consistency of a student's ranking within the group of students against which the student is being compared (see Dependability).

Reliability coefficient A calculated number whose value must be between 0 and 1. The number describes the consistency of the assessment results. The larger the number's magnitude, the more consistent the assessment. For example, if the coefficient value were 1, all students' scores would be expected to rank exactly the same way on retesting.

Report card Summary of student achievement, either formative or summative, describing student progress and development with respect to learner expectations, cognitive ability, and expected behavior.

Rubric A description of a specific level of performance within a performance scale.

Sample A part of a population.

School district A legally constituted collection of institutions, within defined geographic and/or philosophical boundaries, that collaborate in teaching students of less than college age.

Score A specific value in a range of possible values describing the performance of a student.

Scoring key A list of correct answers for selection items or the scoring guide to be followed with scoring or judging responses to constructed response items.

Selection item Test item or task to which the students respond by selecting their answers from choices given: true-false, matching, multiple choice.

Self-assessment An assessment method in which students make and report judgments about their own performance.

Stakeholder Any person legitimately involved in or affected by the evaluation, for example, students, their parents/guardians, teachers, guidance counselors, school psychologists, and others who make decisions that affect the education of the student.

Standard A description of the expected level of performance that describes minimum competence in relation to a critical score or other measure of student performance.

Standard deviation The standard deviation is a calculated number that describes the extent to which scores are dispersed (spread out) from the mean. Nearly all scores are typically within 3 standard deviations of the mean.

Standardized tests Assessment methods, either criterion- or norm-referenced, designed to be administered, scored, and interpreted in the same way regardless of when and where they are administered.

Statistic A summary number typically used to describe a characteristic of a sample and from which inferences about the population represented by the sample are made.

Student evaluation The process of systematically collecting and interpreting information that can be used (1) to inform students, and their parents/guardians where applicable, about the progress they are making toward attaining the knowledge, skills, attitudes, and behaviors to be learned or acquired; and (2) to inform the various personnel who make educational decisions (instructional, diagnostic, placement, promotion, graduation) about students.

Student evaluation system All the procedures—including developing and choosing methods for assessment, collecting assessment information, judging and scoring student performance, summarizing and interpreting results, reporting evaluation findings—and policies that evaluators use to evaluate their students.

Subjective scoring Different scorers and raters may differ on a student's score or rating; most often associated with constructed response assessments (see Objective scoring).

Summative evaluation An evaluation designed to present conclusions about the merit or worth of a student's performance (see Formative evaluation).

Task A single question, problem, or task used to assess a student (see Item).

Utility The extent to which an evaluation will serve the relevant information needs of students, their parents, and other appropriate users.

Validity Related to the purposes of the evaluation, the degree to which inferences drawn about a student's knowledge, skills, attitudes, and behaviors from the results of assessment methods used are correct, trustworthy, and appropriate for making decisions about students.

Variable A characteristic of students that can take on different values: for example, achievement, skill, attitude, and behavior.

Weighting The amount of emphasis given to a particular set of information. For grading purposes, weighting usually entails multiplying all scores for one component (e.g., a test) by a numerical value (e.g., 2) to increase the emphasis it receives over other data (e.g., student homework).

Index

THE STUDENT EVALUATION STANDARDS

Sound student evaluation practices, when applied in all educational settings, should have four basic attributes:

- Propriety
- Utility
- Feasibility
- Accuracy

The Student Evaluation Standards, established by sixteen professional education associations, identifies evaluation principles that, when addressed, should result in improved student evaluations containing the above four attributes.

Dr. Arlen Gullickson, Chair
The Joint Committee on Standards
for Educational Evaluation
The Evaluation Center
Western Michigan University

Corwin Press, Inc.
2455 Teller Road
Thousand Oaks, CA 91320
www.corwinpress.com

JCSEE PR-2002
Approved by the American National Standards Institute as an American National Standard.
Approval date: 6/26/02

Propriety

P Propriety Standards The propriety standards help ensure that student evaluations will be conducted legally, ethically, and with due regard for the well-being of the students being evaluated and other people affected by the evaluation results. These standards are as follows:

P1 Service to Students Evaluations of students should promote sound education principles, fulfillment of institutional missions, and effective student work, so that educational needs of students are served.

P2 Appropriate Policies and Procedures Written policies and procedures should be developed, implemented, and made available, so that evaluations are consistent, equitable, and fair.

P3 Access to Evaluation Information Access to a student's evaluation information should be provided, but limited to the student and others with established legitimate permission to view the information, so that confidentiality is maintained and privacy protected.

P4 Treatment of Students Students should be treated with respect in all aspects of the evaluation process, so that their dignity and opportunities for educational development are enhanced.

P5 Rights of Students Evaluations of students should be consistent with applicable laws and basic principles of fairness and human rights, so that students' rights and welfare are protected.

P6 Balanced Evaluation Evaluations of students should provide information that identifies both strengths and weaknesses, so that strengths can be built upon and problem areas addressed.

P7 Conflict of Interest Conflicts of interest should be avoided, but if present should be dealt with openly and honestly, so that they do not compromise evaluation processes and results.

Utility

U Utility Standards The utility standards help ensure that student evaluations are useful. Useful student evaluations are informative, timely, and influential. Standards that support usefulness are as follows:

U1 Constructive Orientation Student evaluations should be constructive, so that they result in educational decisions that are in the best interest of the student.

U2 Defined Users and Uses The users and uses of a student evaluation should be specified, so that evaluation appropriately contributes to student learning and development.

U3 Information Scope The information collected for student evaluations should be carefully focused and sufficiently comprehensive, so that evaluation questions can be fully answered and the needs of students addressed.

U4 Evaluator Qualifications Teachers and others who evaluate students should have the necessary knowledge and skills, so that evaluations are carried out competently and the results can be used with confidence.

U5 **Explicit Values** In planning and conducting student evaluations, teachers and others who evaluate students should identify and justify the values used to judge student performance, so that the bases for the evaluations are clear and defensible.

U6 **Effective Reporting** Student evaluation reports should be clear, timely, accurate, and relevant, so that they are useful to students, their parents/guardians, and other legitimate users.

U7 **Follow-Up** Student evaluations should include procedures for follow-up, so that students, parents/guardians, and other legitimate users can understand the information and take appropriate follow-up actions.

Feasibility

F **Feasibility Standards** The feasibility standards help ensure that student evaluations can be implemented as planned. Feasible evaluations are practical, diplomatic, and adequately supported. These standards are as follows:

F1 **Practical Orientation** Student evaluation procedures should be practical, so that they produce the needed information in efficient, nondisruptive ways.

F2 **Political Viability** Student evaluations should be planned and conducted with the anticipation of questions from students, their parents/guardians, and other legitimate users, so that their questions can be answered effectively and their cooperation obtained.

F3 **Evaluation Support** Adequate time and resources should be provided for student evaluations, so that evaluations can be effectively planned and implemented, their results fully communicated, and appropriate follow-up activities identified.

Accuracy

A **Accuracy Standards** The accuracy standards help ensure that a student evaluation will produce sound information about a student's learning and performance. Sound information leads to valid interpretations, justifiable conclusions, and appropriate follow-up. These standards are as follows:

A1 **Validity Orientation** Student evaluations should be developed and implemented, so that interpretations made about the performance of a student are valid and not open to misinterpretation.

A2 **Defined Expectations for Students** The performance expectations for students should be clearly defined, so that evaluation results are defensible and meaningful.

A3 **Context Analysis** Student and contextual variables that may influence performance should be identified and considered, so that a student's performance can be validly interpreted.

A4 **Documented Procedures** The procedures for evaluating students, both planned and actual, should be described, so that the procedures can be explained and justified.

A5 **Defensible Information** The adequacy of information gathered should be ensured, so that good decisions are possible and can be defended and justified.

A6 **Reliable Information** Evaluation procedures should be chosen or developed and implemented, so that they provide reliable information for decisions about the performance of a student.

A7 **Bias Identification and Management** Student evaluations should be free from bias, so that conclusions can be fair.

A8 **Handling Information and Quality Control** The information collected, processed, and reported about students should be systematically reviewed, corrected as appropriate, and kept secure, so that accurate judgments can be made.

A9 **Analysis of Information** Information collected for student evaluations should be systematically and accurately analyzed, so that the purposes of the evaluation are effectively achieved.

A10 **Justified Conclusions** The evaluative conclusions about student performance should be explicitly justified, so that students, their parents/guardians, and others can have confidence in them.

A11 **Metaevaluation** Student evaluation procedures should be examined periodically using these and other pertinent standards, so that mistakes are prevented or detected and promptly corrected, and sound student evaluation practices are developed over time.

Guidelines and illustrative cases to assist teachers and others in meeting each of these standards are provided in *The Student Evaluation Standards* (Corwin, 2003). The illustrative cases are based in classrooms that include elementary, secondary, and higher education settings.